ALEX COMFORT M.B., D.Sc.

the JOY of SEX

CROWN PUBLISHERS / NEW YORK

"i like my body when it is with you" is reprinted from
TULIPS & CHIMNEYS by E.E. Cummings, edited by
George James Firmago, by permission of Liveright
Publishing Corporation. Copyright 1923, 1925, and
renewed 1951, 1953 by E.E. Cummings. Copyright ©
1973, 1976 by the Trustees for the E.E. Cummings Trust.
Copyright © 1976 by George James Firmago.

Published by Crown Publishers, New York, New York.
Member of the Crown Publishing Group, a division of
Random House, Inc.
www.randomhouse.com

This edition originally published in Great Britain in 2002 by
Mitchell Beazley, an imprint of Octopus Publishing Group
Ltd. First published in Great Britain by Modset Securities
Ltd. in 1972. Updated and reillustrated edition published in
Great Britain 1991, 1996 by Mitchell Beazley, an imprint of
Octopus Publishing Group Ltd.

Printed in Hong Kong

Library of Congress Cataloging-in-Publication Data is
available upon request.

ISBN 1-4000-4958-X

10 9 8 7 6 5 4 3 2 1

First American Edition

i like my body when it is with your
body. It is so quite new a thing.
Muscles better and nerves more.
i like your body. i like what it does,
i like its hows. i like to feel the spine
of your body and its bones, and the
trembling-firm-smooth ness and which
i will again and again and again kiss, i
like kissing this and that of you, i like,
slowly stroking the, shocking fuzz
of your electric fur, and what-is-it
comes over parting flesh.... And eyes
big love crumbs,

and possibly i like the thrill

of under me you so quite new

e.e.cummings

contents

preface

I am a physician and human biologist for whom the natural history of human sexuality is of as much interest as the rest of human natural history. As with the rest of human natural history, I had notes on it. My wife encouraged me to bring biology into medicine, and my old medical school had no decent textbook to teach a human sexuality course.

JOY was compiled and, very importantly, illustrated, just after the end of that daft and extraordinary non-statute in Western society, the Sexual Official Secrets Act. For at least two hundred years the description, and above all the depiction, of this most familiar and domestic group of activities, and of almost everything associated with them, had been classified. When, in the sixteenth century, Giulio Romano engraved his weightily classical pictures showing sixteen ways of making love, and Aretino wrote poems to go with them, a leading ecclesiastic opined that the artist deserved to be crucified. The public apparently thought otherwise ("Why," said Aretino, "should we not look upon that which pleases us most?") and *Aretin's Postures* have circulated surreptitiously ever since, but even in 1950s Britain the existence of pubic hair was artistically classified: it had to be airbrushed out to provide a smooth and featureless surface.

People today who never experienced the freeze on sexual information won't appreciate the proportions of the transformation when it ended – it was like ripping down the Iron Curtain. My immediate predecessor in writing about domestic sex, Dr Eustace Chesser, was (unsuccessfully) prosecuted for his low-key, unillustrated book *Love Without Fear*, and even in 1972 there was still some remaining doubt whether JOY would be banned by the police.

The main aim of "sexual bibliotherapy" (writing books like this one) was to undo some of the mischief caused by guilt, misinformation, and no-information.

That kind of reassurance is still needed. I have asked various people – chiefly older couples – whether *The Joy of Sex* told them things they did not know, or reassured them about things they knew and already did or would like to do. I have had both answers. One can now read books and see pictures devoted to sexual behavior almost without limitation in democratic countries, but it takes more than 20 years and a turnover of generations to undo centuries of misinformation; and of the material released by the new glasnost about sex, much is anxious or hostile or over the top. People who worried, when the book first came out, if they did some of the things described in it may now worry if they don't do all of them. That we can't help, nor the fact that the same people who went to doctors because of sexual fear and inhibition under the old dispensation now go to doctors complaining of sexual indigestion under the new.

Sexual behavior probably changes remarkably little over the years – sexual revolutions and moral backlashes chiefly affect the degree of frankness or reticence about what people do in private: the main contributor to any sexual revolution in our own time, insofar as it affects behavior, has not been frankness but the advent of reliable contraception, which makes it possible to separate the reproductive and recreational uses of sexuality. Where unanxious books dealing as accurately as possible with the range of sexual behaviors are most valuable is in encouraging the ordinary, sexually active reader – who both wants to enjoy sex and to be responsible about it – and in helping the helping professions (who have sometimes in the past been unhelpful by counseling out of prejudice or out of limited or eccentric personal experience) to avoid causing problems to their clients. It is only recently, as ethology has replaced psychoanalytic theory, that counselors have come to realize that sex, besides being a serious interpersonal matter, is a deeply rewarding form of play (their clients sensed this, but got little encouragement). Children are not encouraged to be embarrassed about their play: adults often have been and are still. So long as play is not hostile, cruel, unhappy, or limiting, they need not be.

One of the most important uses of play is in expressing a healthy awareness of sexual equality. This involves letting both sexes take turns in controlling the game; sex is no longer what men do to women and women are supposed to enjoy. Sexual interaction is sometimes a loving fusion, sometimes a situation where each is a "sex object" – maturity in sexual relationships involves balancing, rather than denying, the personal and the impersonal aspects of physical arousal. Both are essential and built-in to humans. For anyone who is short on either of these elements, play is the way to learn; men learn to stop domineering and trying to perform, women that they can take control in the give and take of the game rather than by nay-saying. If they achieve this, Man and Woman are one another's best friends in the very sparks that they strike from one another.

This book has changed considerably since its first edition, and it will be revised again in the future as knowledge increases. What will not change is the central importance of unanxious, responsible, and happy sexuality in the lives of normal people. For what they need – in a culture which does not learn skills and comparisons in this area of living by watching – is accurate and unbothered information. The availability of this, and public resistance to the minority of disturbed people who for so long limited it, is an excellent test of the degree of liberty and concern in a society, reflected in the now-old injunction to make love, not war. It is a socially relevant test today.

Alex Comfort, M.B. D.SC., 1991

on advanced lovemaking

All of us, bar any physical limitations, are able to dance and sing – after a fashion. This, if you think about it, summarizes the justification for learning to make love. Love, like singing, is something to be taken spontaneously. On the other hand, the difference between Pavlova and the Palais de Danse, or opera and barbershop singing, is much less than the difference between sex as our recent ancestors came to accept it and sex as it can be.

At least we recognize this now (so that instead of worrying if sex is sinful, most people now worry whether they are "getting satisfaction" – one can worry about anything, given the determination). There are now enough books about the basics: the main use of these is to get rid of worries over the normality, possibility, and variety of sexual experience. The people who go to sex counselors are still getting over hang-ups so basic that in past generations the folk tradition would have taken care of them. At least permissiveness in publishing removed some of this cover-up. Our book is slightly different, in that there are now enough people who have the basics and really need hard information (not simply reassurance).

Chef-grade cooking doesn't happen naturally: it starts at the point where people know how to prepare and enjoy food, are curious about it and willing to take trouble preparing it, read recipe hints, and find they are helped by one or two detailed techniques. It's hard to make mayonnaise by trial and error, for instance. Cordon bleu sex, as we define it, is exactly the same situation – the extra one can get from comparing notes, using some imagination, trying way-out or new experiences, when one already is making satisfying love and wants to go on from there.

It is always sad when a love relationship runs aground through non-communication (fear of rejection over some fantasy need, inability to come to terms with aggressive needs through a misplaced idea of tenderness, inability to accept sexuality as play). These hang-ups, plus monotony, are a large part of all five or seven year itches, and, between loving and tolerant people, avoidable.

We shall have four sorts of readers; those who don't fancy it, find it disturbing, and would rather stay the way they are – these should put it down, accept our apologies, and stay the way they are: those who are with the idea, but don't like our choice of techniques – these should remember it's a menu, not a rulebook. We have tried to stay wide open, but it is always difficult to write about things one doesn't enjoy, and we have left out long discussion of very specialized sexual attitudes and things like S and M, which aren't really love or even sex in quite our sense of the word. People who like these know already what they want to try. One of the original aims of this book was to cure the notion, born of non-discussion, that common sex needs are odd or weird. As to the general repertoire, the whole joy of sex-with-love is that there are no rules, so long as you enjoy, and the choice is practically unlimited. This is the way most people will use our notes – as a personal one-couple notebook from which they might get ideas. Then there are the hardy experimentalists, bent on trying absolutely everything. They, too, will do best to read this exactly like a cookbook – except that sex is safer in this respect, between lovers, in that you can't get obese or atherosclerotic on it, or give yourself ulcers. The worst you can get is sore, anxious, or disappointed. Sex, prior to the unwelcome advent of AIDS, was perhaps physically the safest of all human activities (leaving out social repercussions). Hopefully it will be so again. You can have infinite variety to suit every taste. But one needs a steady basic diet of quiet, night-and-morning matrimonial intercourse to stand this experimentation on, simply because, contrary to popular ideas, the more regular sex a couple has the higher the deliberately contrived peaks – just as the more you cook routinely, the better and the more reliable banquets you can stage.

Finally, the people we are addressing are the adventurous and uninhibited lovers who want to find the limits of their ability to enjoy sex. That means we take some things for granted – having intercourse naked and spending time over it; being able and willing to make it last, up to a whole afternoon on occasion; having privacy and washing facilities; not being scared of things like genital kisses; not being obsessed with one sexual trick to the exclusion of all others, and, of course, loving each other.

This book is about love as well as sex as the title implies: you don't get high quality sex on any other basis – either you love each other before you come to want it, or, if you happen to get it, you love each other because of it, or both. No point in arguing this, but just as you can't cook without heat you can't make love without feedback (which may be the reason we say "make love" rather than "make sex"). Sex is the one place where we today can learn to treat people as people. Feedback means the right mixture of stop and go, tough and tender, exertion and affection. This comes with empathy and long mutual knowledge. Anyone who expects to get this in a first attempt with a stranger is an optimist, or a neurotic – if they do, it is what used to be called love at first sight, and isn't expendable. "skill", or variety, is no substitute. Also one can't teach tenderness.

This is a book about valid sexual behaviors, plus a certain amount about how and why they work. It isn't a dictionary: in particular we've avoided a lot of the name-entries attached to particular sorts of performance at the start of the twentieth century – the reason is that they are largely out of date. Rather than sticking on labels like narcissism or sadomasochism, biologists and psychiatrists now work by looking at actual behaviors and seeing what use they are or what they signify. Lump names are a handy shorthand, but they tend to be offputting, especially when very general human behaviors get a label which makes them sound like an illness, and they tend to trigger pointless collector's-piece arguments, for example, whether "women are naturally masochistic" because they get penetrated rather than do the penetrating.

We haven't started with a short lecture on the biology and psychology of human sex: instead we've put a little about it into the various entries. Most people now know that human "sexuality" starts at birth and runs continuously from mother–child to man–woman relations, that it involves some periods of programmed anxiety about the genitals ("castration fears") which probably served originally to stop young apes from falling foul of their fathers, but which, in man, are building stones for a lot of other adult behaviors; and that the wide range of human sex needs of all kinds controlled by this unique developmental background – long childhood, close mother–child contact but a taboo on mother–child or father–child sex, close pair-bonding which centers in sexual play, the way bird pair-formation centers in nest-building and display (this is the phenomenon more often described as love), and so on. Without going into details, we've mentioned throughout the book how parts of this human background fit into the pattern of what humans enjoy sexually. Most human sex behaviors "mean" a whole range of different things (often described as "overdetermined": for examples of what this means in practice see what we've written about *Clothes*, for instance).

A little theory makes sex more interesting, more comprehensible, and less scary – too much is a put-down, especially as you're likely to get it out of perspective and become a spectator of your own performance. If you have really troublesome hangups you need an expert to hold the mirror for you and go personally into what they mean – self-adhesive labels are actively unhelpful. All humans are sadistic, narcissistic, masochistic, bisexual, and what have you – labels are for fashion victims. Ignore them. What matters is whether any of the behaviors in which you engage are bothering you or other people – if so, they are a useful pointer to what the problem is, but no more than that.

The starting point of all lovemaking is close bodily contact. Love has been defined as the harmony of two souls and the contact of two epidermes. It is also, from our infancy, the starting point of human relationships and needs. Our culture ("Anglo-Saxon"), after several centuries of intense taboos on many such contacts – between friends, between males – which are used by other cultures, has cut down "intimacy" based on bodily contact to parent–child and lover–lover situations. We're getting over this taboo, or at least the part which has spilled over into baby-raising and explicit lovemaking, but coupled with our other cultural reservation, which says that play and fantasy are only safe for children, it has dealt us a bad hand for really full and personal sex. Our idea of sex wouldn't be recognizable to some other cultures, though our range of choice is the widest ever. For a start, it's over-genital: "sex" for our culture means putting the penis in the vagina. Our entire skin is a genital organ. As to touching, proximity and so on, see Desmond Morris's brilliant account in *Intimate Behavior*, which catalogued our hangups. Good sex is about the only adult remedy for these.

There isn't too much point in crying over cultural spilt milk. Our sex repertoire has to be geared to us as we are, not to Trobriand Islanders (who have their own, different hangups).

We need extensive sex play which is centered in intercourse, and in doing things. At the same time, we might as well plan our menu so that we learn to use the rest of our equipment. That includes our whole skin surface, our feelings of identity, aggression, and so on, and all of our fantasy needs. Luckily, sex behavior in humans is enormously elastic (it has had to be, or we wouldn't be here) and also nicely geared to help us express most of the needs which society or our upbringing have corked up. Elaboration in sex is something we need rather specially (though it isn't confined to our sort of society), and it has the advantage that if we really make it work it makes us more, not less, receptive to each other as people. This is the answer to anyone who thinks that conscious effort to increase our sex range is "mechanical" or a substitute for treating each other as people – we may start that way, but it's an excellent entry to learning that we are people – probably the only one our sort of society can really use at the moment. There may be other places we can learn to express all of ourselves, and do it mutually, but there aren't many.

Those are our assumptions. Granted this feedback and mutual exploration, there are two modes of sex, the duet and the solo, and a good concert alternates between them. The duet is a cooperative effort aiming at simultaneous orgasm, or at least one orgasm each, and complete, untechnically-planned release. This in fact needs skill, and can be built up from more calculated "love-play" until doing the right thing for both of you becomes fully automatic. This is the basic sexual meal. The solo, by contrast, is when one partner is the player and the other the instrument. The aim of the player is to produce results on the other's pleasure experience as extensive, unexpected, and generally wild as his or her skill allows   to blow them out of themselves. The player doesn't lose control, though he or she can get wildly excited by what is happening to the other. The instrument does lose control – in fact, with a responsive instrument and a skillful performer, this is the concerto situation – if it ends in an uncontrollable ensemble, so much the better. All the elements of music and dance are involved – rhythm, mounting tension, tantalization, even actual aggression: "I'm like the executioner," said the lady in the Persian poem, "but where he inflicts intolerable pain I will only make you die of pleasure." There is indeed an element of aggression or infliction in the solo mode, which is why some lovers dislike it and others overdo it, but no major lovemaking is complete without some solo passages.

The antique idea of the woman as passive and the man as performer used to ensure that he would show off playing solos on her, and early marriage manuals perpetuated this idea. Today, she is herself the soloist par excellence, whether in getting him excited to start with, or in controlling him and showing off all her skills. In fact there is only one really unmusical situation, and that is the reverse of a real solo, where one uses the other to obtain satisfaction, without any attempt at mutuality. True, one may say, "do it yourself this time," as a quick finish, but it is no more than that.

In the Old World, extended solo techniques have never quite died as a male skill: in Europe at one time, calculated solo skill among women was supposed to be limited to prostitutes. Now it is on the way back, starting half-heartedly with "petting to climax", but getting today to be a polite accomplishment: we shall probably have extension courses soon. This, as usual, will likely go too far and become a substitute for full, let-go intercourse – whereas in fact it's a preparation, supplement, overture, bridging operation, tailpiece, interlude. The solo-given orgasm is unique, however – neither bigger nor smaller in either sex than in a full duet, but different. We've heard both sexes call it "sharper but not so round", and most people who have experienced both like to alternate them; it is also quite different from self-stimulation, which most people like occasionally, too. Trying to say how they differ is a little like describing wines. Differ they do, however, and much depends on cultivating and alternating them.

Solo devices are not, of course, necessarily separate from intercourse. Apart from leading into it, there are many coital solos – for the woman astride, for example – while mutual masturbation or genital kisses can be fully-fledged duets. Nor is it anything to do with "clitoral" versus "vaginal" orgasm (this is only a crass anatomical way of trying to verbalize a real difference), since the man feels the same distinction, and you can get a roaring solo orgasm from the skin of the fingertips, the breasts, the soles of the feet, or the earlobes of a receptive woman (less commonly extra-genitally in the man). Coition which ought to be mutual but gives a solo feeling (to her) is what people who talk about "clitoral orgasm" are trying as a rule to verbalize. Solo-response can be electrifyingly extreme in the quietest people. Skillfully handled by someone who doesn't stop for yells of murder, but does know when to stop, a woman can get orgasm after orgasm, and a man can be kept hanging just short of climax to the limit of human endurance.

Top-level enjoyment doesn't have to be varied, it just often is. In fact, being stuck rigidly with one sex technique usually means anxiety. In this book, we have not, for example, gone heavily on things like coital postures. The common positions are now familiar to most people from writing and pictures if not from trial – the more extreme ones, as a rule, should be spontaneous, but few of them have marked advantages. Moreover, the technique of straight intercourse, which needs a suspension of self-observation, doesn't lend itself to treatment in writing, except for elementary students. This explains the apparent emphasis in our book on extras – the "sauces and pickles". Most of these are psychologically and biologically geared to cover specific human needs, often left over from a "civilized" childhood. Individuals who, through a knot in their psyche, are obliged to live on sauce and pickle only are unfortunate in missing the most sustaining part of the meal – kinks and exclusive obsessions in sex are very like living exclusively on horseradish sauce through allergy to beef; fear of horseradish sauce as indigestible, unnecessary, and immature is another hangup, namely puritanism. As to our choice of needs and/or problems, we've based it on a good many years of listening to people.

In writing descriptively about sex, it is hard not to be solemn, however unsolemnly we play in bed. In fact, one of the things still missing from the essence of sexual freedom is the unashamed ability to use sex as play. In the past, psychoanalytic ideas of maturity were nearly as much to blame as old style moralisms about what is normal or perverse. We are all immature and have anxieties and aggressions. Coital play, like dreaming, is probably a programmed way of dealing acceptably with these, just as children express their fears and aggressions in games. If they play aggressive games, out of jealousy of their little brother or the opposite sex, we don't call that sadism: adults are unfortunately afraid of playing games, of dressing up, of acting scenes. It makes them self-conscious: something horrid might get out.

Bed is the place to play all the games you have ever wanted to play, at the play-level – if adults could become less self-conscious about such "immature" needs, we should have fewer deeply anxious and committed fetishists creating a sense of community to enable them to do their thing without feeling isolated. We heard of a frogman who used to make his wife sleep in rubber bedsheets; he had to become a frogman for real, because dressing in a diving suit for kicks was embarrassing and made him look odd. If we were able to transmit the sense of play which is essential to a full, enterprising, and healthily immature view of sex between committed people, we would be performing a mitzvah: people who play flagellation games and are excited by them bother nobody, provided they don't turn off a partner who finds the scenario frightening. People who enact similar aggressions outside the bedroom are apt to end up in prison or a psychiatric ward. The aim of this book is pleasure, not psychiatry, but we suspect that the two coincide. Play is one function of sexual elaboration – playfulness is a part of love which could well be the major contribution of the 60s-generation to human happiness. Hence the association with pregenital and immature sauces and pickles.

But still the main dish is loving, unselfconscious intercourse – long, frequent, varied, ending with both parties satisfied, but not so full they can't face another light course, and another meal in a few hours. The *pièce de résistance* is the good old face-to-face matrimonial, the finishing-off position, with mutual orgasm, and starting with a full day or night of ordinary tenderness. Other ways of making love are special in various ways, and the changes of timbre are infinitely varied – complicated ones are for special occasions, or special uses like holding off an over-quick male orgasm, or are things which, like pepper steak, are stunning once a year but not dietary.

If you don't like our repertoire or if it doesn't square with yours, never mind. The aim of *The Joy of Sex* is to stimulate your imagination. You can preface your own ideas with "this is how we play it," and play it your way. But by that time, when you'll have tried all your own creative fantasies, you won't need books. Sex books can only suggest techniques to encourage you to experiment.

There are after all only two "rules" in good sex, apart from the obvious one of not doing things which are silly, antisocial, or dangerous. One is "don't do anything you don't really enjoy," and the other is "find out your partner's needs and don't balk them if you can help it." In other words, a good giving and taking relationship depends on a compromise (so does going to a show – if you both want the same thing, fine: if not, take turns, and don't let one partner always dictate). This can be easier than it sounds because, unless your partner wants something you find actively off-putting, real lovers get a reward not only from their own satisfactions but from seeing the other respond and become satisfied. Most wives who don't like Chinese food will eat it occasionally for the pleasure of seeing a sinophile husband enjoy it, and vice versa. Partners who won't do this over specific sex needs are usually balking, not because they've tried it and it's a turn-off (many experimental dishes turn out nicer than you expected), but simply through ignorance of the range of human needs, plus being scared if these include things like aggression, cultivating extragenital sensation, or play-acting, which the last half-century's social mythology pretended weren't there. Reading a full list of the unscheduled accessory sex behaviors which some normal people find helpful might be thought a necessary preliminary to any extended sex relationship, particularly marriage if you really intend to stay with it, but so far the books haven't helped in this respect. If anything, they've scared people rather than instructed them.

Couples should match up their needs and preferences (though people don't find these out at once). You won't get to some of our suggestions or understand them until you've learned to respond. It's a mistake to run so long as walking is such an enchanting and new experience, and you may be happy pedestrians who match automatically. Most people who marry rightly prefer to try themselves out and play themselves in. Where a rethink really helps is at the point where you've got used to each other socially (sex needs aren't the only ones which need matching up between people who live together) and feel that the surface needs repolishing. If you think that sexual relations are overrated, it does need repolishing, and you haven't paid enough attention to the wider use of your sexual equipment as a way of communicating totally. The traditional expedient at the point where the surface gets dull is to trade in the relationship and start all over in an equally uninstructed attempt with someone else, on the offchance of getting a better match-up by random choice. This is emotionally wasteful, and you usually repeat the same mistakes.

One specific group of readers deserves special note. If you are disabled in any way, don't stop reading. A physical disability is not an obstacle to fulfilling sex. In counseling disabled people, one repeatedly finds that the real disability isn't a mechanical problem, but a mistaken idea that there is only one "right" – or enjoyable – way to have sex. The best technique with this book is probably to go through it with your partner marking off the things you can do. Then pick something appealing which you think you can't quite do, and see if there is a strategy you can develop together. Talking to other couples where one partner has a problem similar to yours is another resource.

We suggest couples can either read the book together or (perhaps even better), read it separately, marking passages for the other partner's attention. This works wonders if – as is often the case – you don't really talk easily about sexual needs, or are afraid of sounding tactless.

the implications of AIDS

When the original edition of this book was first written, in the early 1970s, sex was an extremely safe occupation, and any hazards attending it were social and emotional. The major venereal diseases, especially syphilis, which had caused death and disability for the previous 400 years, were curable: those which had replaced them, nonspecific urethritis and herpes, though troublesome, were not life-threatening. This picture was changed in the late 1980s by the introduction to Western societies of AIDS – acquired immunodeficiency syndrome. The arrival of this disease totally alters the sexual landscape. There is a full discussion of AIDS on page 188. Read it, preferably before you read anything else in this book.

AIDS, caused by the infectious agent HIV (human immunodeficiency virus) first came to light with the death of five gay men in Los Angeles in 1981, and was initially labelled a gay man's disease. (We now know that pockets of the virus had been around in Africa for decades, and it is generally agreed that the virus has its origins in the African continent.) Homosexuals were thought to have been an easy target for HIV because they had more sexual partners and more anal sex than straight men, and for many the disease became a justification for homophobia. But it quickly became apparent that hemophiliacs receiving blood products, and intravenous drug users were at high risk. It was five years into the epidemic before the heterosexual community was finally awakened from its complacency by stark official warnings that anyone, regardless of race, sexual orientation, or social group, having unprotected sex – without a condom – was at risk of catching the virus.

Despite record new levels in the rate of HIV infections (36.1 million people worldwide were estimated to be living with HIV/AIDS at the beginning of the twenty first century), many now see AIDS as yesterday's disease. They have been lulled into a false sense of security by the advances in drug treatments that appear to slow down the rate the virus progresses. But these treatments are in their infancy, and the problems of adverse side effects and drug-resistant strains of HIV are still very real, making the need to practice safe sex still of essential importance for all. However, if we heed this advice, there is no reason why we should lose out on the joy of sex.

ingredients

love

We use the same word for man–woman, mother–child,
child–parent, and I–mankind relations – rightly, because they
are a continuous spectrum. In talking about sexual relations, it
seems right to apply it to any relationship in which there is
mutual tenderness, respect, and consideration – from a total
interdependence where the death of one maims the other for
years, to an agreeable night together. The intergrades are all
love, all worthy, all part of human experience. Some meet the
needs of one person, some of another – or of the same person at
different times. That's really the big problem of sexual ethics,
and it's basically a problem of self-understanding and of
communication. You can't assume that your "conditions of
love" are applicable to, or accepted by, any other party; you
can't assume that these won't be changed quite unpredictably in
both of you by the experience of loving; you can't necessarily
know your own mind. If you are going to love, these are risks
you have to take, and they don't depend simply on whether or
not you have sex together – though that is such a potentially
overwhelming experience that tradition is right in pinpointing
it. Sometimes two people know each other very well, or think
they've worked things out by discussion, and they may be right.
But even so, if it's dignifiable by the name of love, it's
potentially an open-ended experience. Tradition has tried to cut
the casualties by laying down all kinds of schedules of morality,
but these never work 100 percent. Nor are they of much use in
classifying the merits of different kinds of relationship.
Romantic sentimentalism made a whole generation see "love"
as a kind of takeover bid by one individual for another. Those in
revolt from this are, like Casanova, so hung up on no hangups
that they won't accept the essential openness of a real
relationship between people.

love

*...the essential openness
of a real relationship between
people...*

If sexual love can be – and it is – the supreme human experience, it must be also a bit hazardous. It can give us our best and our worst moments. In this respect, it's like mountain climbing – over-timid people miss the whole experience; reasonably balanced and hardy people accept the risks for the rewards, but realize that there's a difference between this and being foolhardy. Love, moreover, involves someone else's neck beside your own. At least you can make as sure as may be that you don't exploit or injure someone – you don't take a novice climbing and abandon them halfway up when things get difficult. Getting them to sign a form of consent before they start isn't an answer either. There was a great deal to be said for the English Victorian idea of not being a cad ("person devoid of finer or gentlemanly feelings"). A cad can be of either sex.

Marriage between two rival actor-managers, each trying to produce the other regardless, isn't love. The relationship between a prostitute and a casual client where, for reasons they don't quite get, real tenderness and respect occur, is.

fidelity

Fidelity, infidelity, jealousy, and so on. We've deliberately not gone into the ethics of lifestyle. The facts are that few of us go through life with sexual experience confined to one partner only. What suits a particular couple depends on their needs, situation, anxieties, and so on. These needs are a particularly delicate problem in communication: if mutual comprehension is complete and ongoing, you can count yourselves lucky. Active deception always hurts a relationship. Complete frankness which is aimed to avoid guilt or as an act of aggression against a partner can do the same. The real problem arises from the fact that sexual relations can be anything, for different people and on different occasions, from a game to a total fusion of identities; the heartaches arise when each partner sees it differently.

There is no sexual relationship which doesn't involve responsibility because there are two or more people involved: anything which, as it were, militantly excludes a partner is hurtful, yet to be whole people we have at some point to avoid total fusion with each other – "I am I and you are you, and neither of us is on earth to live up to the other's expectations." People who communicate sexually have to find their own fidelities. All we can suggest is that you discuss them, so that at least you know where each of you stands.

fidelity
To be whole people, we have at some point to avoid total fusion.

safe sex

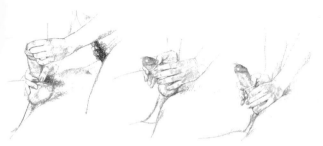

safe sex

*Always use a condom before
any act of vaginal or oral sex,
and always remove it – and
wash the penis – before the
erection subsides.*

The concept of safe sex surfaced only with the outbreak of
AIDS. The message was to avoid anal sex altogether, and reduce
risk by rejecting any other form of sex without a condom. The
facts are that, if neither partner is HIV positive, the whole range
of close-contact sexual behavior is safe – if either is, virtually
none is safe. Protected vaginal intercourse is considered the
least risky, unprotected receptive anal intercourse the most
hazardous. But how do you know your sexual partner is not
HIV positive? People often do not realize they have been
exposed to the virus, which can take up to 10 years to develop
into AIDS, during which time the person infected may show no
symptoms of the disease. And even if they think they might be
infected, HIV can take up to three months to be detectable in a
blood test, so having the test too soon could result in a false
negative (see page 190). Self-defense rules out unprotected sex,
including oral sex, with chance acquaintances anywhere. If you
are with a long-term partner, you need to be aware of other
avenues of risk for either of you, such as intravenous drug use
or unprotected intercourse with other people.
  If you are not already infected, make sure that bodily fluids
that might carry the virus – semen, blood, and vaginal
secretions – have no chance of entering the body through
broken skin such as a cut or abrasion anywhere on the body.
Although women are eight times more likely to become infected
from an infected man than the other way round, they are still
able to pass on the HIV virus through vaginal secretions,
menstrual blood, and cells in the vaginal and anal walls.
Practising safe sex not only reduces the risk of transmitting or
contracting AIDS, but also other sexually transmitted diseases
such as chlamydia, gonorrhea, herpes, and hepatitis B and C.

At a cautious view, no sex with a known HIV-positive person is really "safe". Safe sex is designed to reduce the risk with unknown partners. It represents the minimum reasonable caution, and could reduce the spread of HIV statistically – though if it fails in your case, for you the incidence is 100 percent.

Those who are known to be HIV positive present their partners with the greatest problem: it's an agonizing decision to withhold sex or to run the risk of getting AIDS. Counselors on AIDS hotlines will have the most recent experience to draw on and can help you both to deal with the problem.

tenderness

This, in fact, is what the whole book is about. It doesn't exclude extremely violent games (though many people neither need nor want these), but it does exclude clumsiness, heavy-handedness, lack of feedback, spitefulness, and non-rapport generally. Tenderness is shown fully in the way you touch each other. What it implies at root is a constant awareness of what your partner is feeling, plus the knowledge of how to heighten that feeling, gently, toughly, slowly, or fast, and this only comes from an inner state of mind between you. No really tender person can just turn over and go to sleep. Many if not most inexperienced men, and some women, are just naturally clumsy – either through haste, through anxiety, or through lack of sensing how the other sex feels. Men in general are harder-skinned than women – don't grab breasts, stick fingers into the vagina, handle female skin as if it were your own, or (and this goes for both sexes) misplace bony parts of your anatomy. More women respond to very light than to very heavy stimulation – just brushing pubic or skin hairs will usually do far more than a whole-hand grab. At the same time, don't be frightened – neither of you is made of glass. Women by contrast often fail to use enough pressure, especially in handwork, though the light, light variety is a sensation on its own. Start very gently, making full use of the skin surface, and work up. Stimulus toleration in any case increases with sexual excitement until even hard blows can become excitants (though not for everyone). This loss of pain sense disappears almost instantly with orgasm, so don't go on too long, and be extra gentle as soon as he or she has come.

If we could teach tenderness, most of this book would be superseded by intuition. If you are really heavy-handed, a little practice with inanimate surfaces, dress fastenings, and so on will help. Male strength is a turn-on in sex, but it isn't expressed in clumsy handwork, bear hugs, and brute force – at least not as starters. If there is a problem here, remember you both can talk. Few people want to be in bed on any terms with a person who isn't basically tender, and most people are delighted to be in bed with the right person who is. The ultimate test is whether you can bear to find the person there when you wake up. If you are actually pleased, then you're onto the right thing.

tenderness
What it implies is a
constant awareness of what
your partner is feeling.

women (by her for him)

Women, like men, have direct physical responses, sure, but these are different (breasts and skin first, please, not a direct grab at the clitoris) and can't be short-circuited. It matters to us who is doing what, far more than it does to most men. The fact that, unlike you, we can't be visibly turned off and lose erection often confuses men into hurrying things or missing major resources. It isn't true that nudity, erotica, etc don't excite women – probably the difference is that they aren't overriding things. Is it fair, I wonder, to give a simple instance? You can make orgiastically satisfactory love with a near stranger in half an hour flat. But please don't think for that reason that you can do the same for a woman who loves you personally if, at the end of the half-hour, you turn over and go straight to sleep. Granted this, however, there are common reactions.

We seem to be less heavily programmed than you for specific turn-ons, but, once we see one of these working on a man we care about, we soon program it into our own response, and can be less rigid and more experimental because of this ability.

Often, if women seem underactive, it's because they're scared of doing the wrong thing with that particular man, like touching up his penis when in fact he's trying not to ejaculate – tell us if you see us at a loss. The penis isn't a "weapon" for us so much as a shared possession – it's less the size than its personality, unpredictable movements, and moods which make up the turn-on.

Another important thing is the tough-tender mixture: obviously strength is a turn-on, but clumsiness (elbows in eyes, twisted fingers, etc.) is the dead opposite. You never get anywhere by clumsy brutality; however brutal good lovemaking sometimes looks, the turn-on is strength-skill-control, not large bruises: and the ability to be tender with it. Some people ask "Tough or tender?" but the mood shifts so fast you've got to be able to sense it. Surely it's possible – because some lovers do it – to read this balance from the feel of the woman. No obsessive views about reciprocity – who comes on top, etc, does in fact even out during the passing of time: there can be long spells when one enjoys and is happy to let him do the work, and others when you need to control everything yourself, and take an extra kick from seeing how you make him respond.

Women aren't any more "masochistic" than men – if they've knuckled under in the past it's only through social pressures. If they're sadistic, they don't always act it out in bed by wearing spurs and cracking a whip. Men have a real advantage here in the constructive use of play (and can help women to act it out, too). Since we all have some aggressions, good sex can be wildly violent, but still never cruel. A little frightening helps some people sometimes.

As for sexual equality, nobody can possibly be a good lover without regarding their partner as a person and an equal. That is really all there is to be said.

women

Nobody can be a good lover if he doesn't regard women as (a) people and (b) equals.

Our sense of smell is the keener – don't oversaturate early on with masculine odors; just before orgasm is probably the time for full odor contact. Our own smell excites us as well as yours.

The sort of hand- and mouthwork which men like varies enormously. Some like it very rough, some hate it anything but extremely gentle, others in between. There is no way for a woman to tell except by asking and being told – so it's up to the man to say what he likes, or he may get the opposite.

Some men are extraordinarily passive, or unimaginative, or inhibited, and – oddly – when they are any of these things, we do not become correspondingly aggressive. We may long to do things and feel thoroughly frustrated, but we won't dare show it in most cases. So a woman's lovemaking will only be as good as her partner's, and, more important, she will resent any man who is unexciting, not only because he is unexciting, but also because she will know she has been unexciting, too.

Finally, a man should never presume that what excites one woman sexually will work just as well on another woman. Women probably do differ sexually rather more than men because of the greater complexity of their sexual apparatus (breasts, skin, and so on, as well as pussy). Never assume you don't need to relearn for each person. This is true for a woman with a new man, but perhaps a little less so.

men (by him for her)

Men often wish that women's sexuality was like theirs, which it isn't. Male sexual response is far brisker and more automatic: it is triggered easily by things, like putting a coin in a vending machine. Consequently, women and parts of women provide automatic sexual stimulus for men which can make women feel like objects. Your clothes, breasts, odor, etc, aren't what he loves instead of you – simply the things he needs in order to set sex in motion to express love. Women seem to find this hard to understand. Second, most though not all male feeling is ultimately centered in the last inch of the penis (though you can, if you start intelligently, teach him female-type sensitivity all over his skin surface). And, unlike yours, his sexuality depends on a positive performance – he has to be turned on to erection, and not turned off, in order to function; he can't be passively "taken" in a neutral way. This matters intensely to men at a biological and personal level. It explains why men are emphatically penis-centered and tend to start with genital play, probably before you are ready, and when you would rather wait to get in the mood. Genital approach is how men get into the mood.

You need to understand these reactions, as he needs to understand yours. A woman's concern about being a sex object misses the point – sure the woman and the various parts of her are sex objects, but most men ideally would wish to be treated

piecemeal in the same way. Thus, the most valued thing, from you, in actual lovemaking is intuition of these object reactions, and direct initiative – starting the plays, taking hold of the penis, giving genital kisses ahead of being asked – being an initiator, a user of your stimulatory equipment. This is hard to put in simple terms; it is what is meant by "the divine gift of lechery" – the art of sensing turn-ons and going along with them for the partner's response. It isn't the same for the two sexes because male turn-ons are concrete, while many female turn-ons are situational and atmospheric.

Personal folklore apart, what the male turn-on equipment requires is the exact reverse of a virgin or a passively recipient instrument – not a demand situation, as that in itself can threaten a turn-off because of feelings of inadequacy, but a skill situation; I can turn you on and turn myself on in doing so, and from that point we play it both ways and together. You can't of course control your turn-ons any more than he can, but it helps if a woman has some male-type object reactions, like being excited by the sight of a penis, or hairy skin, or by the man stripping, or by physical kinds of play (just as it helps if the man has some sense of atmosphere). It's the active woman who understands his reactions, plays on them, and leads them out, while keeping her own, who is the ideal lover.

men
The "divine gift of lechery"
makes the ideal lover – both
ways round.

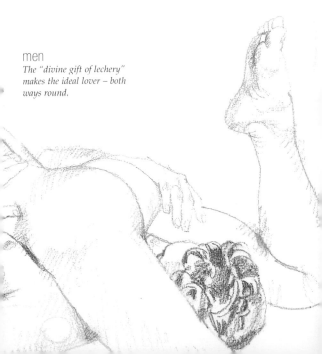

nakedness

The normal state for lovers who take their work at all seriously, at least as a basic requisite – subject to the reservations under *Clothes*. They don't so much start clothed, and shed what they must, as start naked, and add any extras they need.

Nakedness doesn't mean lack of ornament. A woman may take off all her clothes, but put on all her jewels – the only practical need, as with wrist watches, is to see they don't catch or scratch. This is for daylight; it is difficult to sleep in them. For night, probably increase in the value of lovemaking is the main reason that most people now sleep naked. The only exception may be after; warm bodies tend to stick, and a blotter worn by one or other can add to comfort. We find we spend more and more of our time together naked or wearing the enhancing minimum. It affects our choice of clothes and of, for example, nonclammy chairs.

Nudists incidentally used to be associated with health fanatics enjoying a strict regime of cold showers and vigorous sports. Now, thank goodness, a more relaxed attitude prevails. Today, nudity is natural, not a ritual.

Organized "nudism" in most countries is a family affair. This is probably a good idea. For biological reasons which we've hinted at elsewhere (see *Penis, Vulva, Children*), the nudity of one's own parents can be worrying to children and shouldn't be overdone. There is accordingly a lot to be said for the opportunity to look at men and women in general under unforced conditions, and without programmed incest and dominance anxieties: not "father is bigger than I am" but "all men are bigger than I am, and one day I shall be a man." It is the discharge of residual adult anxiety of this sort about our acceptability and competitive status which probably makes group nudity so relaxing, rather than the opportunity of getting sunburned, and explains why it acts as a lay sacrament. Career nudists at a first meeting do have the openness of hippies or Quakers, though they quarrel a fair amount over dogma. You should be able to pick a naturist club to taste – they at least give facilities for open-air nakedness which are hard to organize at home.

nakedness
The normal state for lovers who take their work at all seriously.

cassolette
The natural perfume of
a woman is her greatest
sexual asset after her beauty.

exhibitionism

Most people from babyhood get a kick (though not in front of adults) out of showing their genitals to the opposite sex – they are, after all, some of the best things we've got, and showing them to a partner is the start of better things. For a variety of reasons, some adults can get their sex in no other way and show their genitalia to strangers. This would be an unrewarding activity if people weren't so shocked by it. Society should consider it a disability rather than a crime, as for the most part exhibitionists do not intend harm.

cassolette

French for *perfume box*. The natural perfume of a clean woman: her greatest sexual asset after her beauty (some would say greater than that). It comes from the whole of her – hair, skin, breasts, armpits, genitals, and the clothing she has worn: it is her own signature scent, and no two women are the same. Men have a natural perfume, too, which women are aware of, but, while a man can be infatuated with a woman's personal perfume, women on the whole tend to notice if a man smells right or wrong. Wrong means not so much unpleasant as intangibly not for them. Often their awareness of a man includes conditioned extras like tobacco.

Because it is so important, a woman needs to guard her own personal perfume as carefully as her looks and learn to use it as part of her powers of attraction as skillfully as she uses the rest of her body. Smoking doesn't help this. Her perfume can be a long-range weapon (nothing seduces a man more reliably, and this can happen subliminally without his knowing it), but at the same time a skillful man can read it, if he is an olfactory type and if he knows her, to tell when she is excited.

Susceptibility and consciousness of human clean perfumes vary in both sexes. Whether these are inborn differences, like inability to smell cyanide, or whether they are due to unconscious blocking-out we don't know. Some children can't understand the point of blind man's buff because they know by smell who is touching them: some women can smell that they are pregnant. Men can't smell some chemicals related to musk unless they have a shot of female sex hormone. There is probably a whole biological signal mechanism here which we are only just starting to unravel. Far more human loves and antipathies are based on smell than our deodorant-and-aftershave culture admits. Many people, especially women, say that when it's a question of bed or not-bed, they let their noses lead them.

Women have the keener sense of smell, but men respond to it more as an attractant. In lovemaking, the note changes in regular order, from the totality of skin and *gousset* to her "excited" note, then to her full genital odor, then, when intercourse has begun, to a different scent. Finally, the seminal odor will appear in her breath and trigger the next bout.

Many women shave their armpit hair, conditioned as they are by the idea that hairlessness is sexy. Opinions are divided on this one – fashion dictates armpits should be bare, but in my opinion shaving is simply ignorant vandalism. Hairs catch a woman's natural scent, which is irresistible to a man.

This could be played as an argument for more body hair in general, but men's facial hair doesn't have the day-to-day importance of a woman's little tufts. These are antennae and powderpuffs to introduce herself in a room, or in lovemaking. They are there to brush the man's lips with; he can do the same more circumspectly. Kissing deeply in the armpit leaves a partner's perfume with you. In the genital kiss, start with the lips covered, then brush the closed lips, then open her: when she gives the kiss to a man, she proceeds in the same order. It's the fullest way to become aware of her as a presence, even before you start to touch.

deodorant

Banned absolutely, the only permitted deodorant is soap and water, although the unfortunates who sweat profusely may well have problems. A mouthful of aluminum chloride in an armpit is one of the biggest disappointments bed can afford, it and a truly deodorized woman would be another – like a deodorized carnation.

Cleanliness is another matter. Accordingly, don't give in to sales talk, unless you find that a so-called "intimate deodorant" enhances a natural note which pleases you. Wash, and leave it at that. She says: "some men should use deodorants if they can't learn to wash." See *Cassolette, Mouth music*.

vulva

As magic as the penis, and to many males slightly scary: it looks like a castrating wound and bleeds regularly, it swallows the penis and regurgitates it limp, it can probably bite, and so on. Luckily, few of these biologically programmed anxieties survive closer acquaintance, but they are involved in most male hangups. Prudes treat it as if it were radioactive – "all magic," said a Papuan wizard, "radiates from it as fingers do from a hand," and a lot of female put-downs throughout history grew from this kind of Freudian undergrowth.

Sensitive in all its parts – the phallic-minded male is inclined to make a reassuring rush for the clitoris. Lovers should learn early on to watch one another masturbate – few women enjoy excessive clitoral emphasis at the start. Length of labia, size, and tightness of the opening make little difference to performance –

position relative to the male pubic bone makes more: some lovers only get really good apposition in one or two postures, though usually the tension produced by movement and pulling on the labia in intercourse more than makes up for this. Normally slightly moist, or women would squeak when they walk, the vulva wets more or less copiously with sexual excitement.

Any staining or offensive discharge indicates infection (usually with trichomonads or yeasts) in the vagina, and needs treating. The normal vulval odor varies greatly between women and between times, but should always be pleasant and sexually exciting.

Whether or not your lover has ever explored a woman's pussy in detail, with fingers, eyes, and tongue, make sure he explores yours. Learn to kiss with it – you have two mouths to his one.

For care and maintenance, see *Bidet, Cassolette*. Don't as a rule douche – wash.

Hide-and-seek with the woman's pubic triangle is one of the oldest human games. See *Clothes, Chastity* belt. Cultivate the cunning use of a really practical g-string.

vulva

Whether or not your lover has ever explored a woman's pussy in detail, make sure he explores yours.

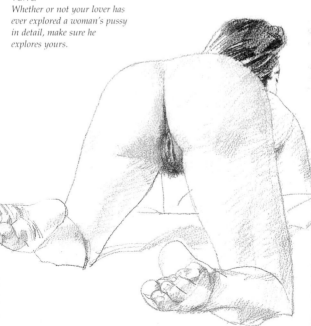

vulva

Hide and seek with the woman's pubic triangle is one of the oldest human games.

mons pubis

The decorative fat-pad over the female pubic bone which acts as a buffer in face-to-face intercourse and, more important, serves to transmit sensation to the rest of the area when it moves. Many men are not aware, if they are oversold on direct clitoris stimulation, that most women can be brought to orgasm simply by holding this gently in the cupped hand and kneading or shaking it, before, without, or as well as putting a finger in the vulva (see *Pubic hair*).

You can either grasp it (it exactly fits the palm) or rest the heel of your hand on it while using the fingers on the labia, or you can cup the whole area, mons and closed labia, in your palm and fingers. Practice seeing how much sensation you can produce with your partner lying completely closed.

breasts

"In our maturer years," wrote Darwin, "when an object of vision is presented to us which bears any similitude to the form of the female bosom . . . we feel a general glow of delight which seems to influence all our senses, and if the object be not too large we experience an attraction to embrace it with our lips as we did in early infancy the bosom of our mothers." Breasts are the natural second target, but often the first one we reach. Just how sensitive they are, in men as well as in women, varies enormously – size is unimportant, as with other sexual organs. Some don't answer at all, even in the emphatically non-frigid;

some answer to extremely gentle touches, some to very rough handling (but they are sensitive structures – don't let your residual anger at having been weaned get the better of your commonsense).

Round and round the nipple with the tongue tip or the glans, soft kneading with both hands, gentle biting, and sucking gently like a baby are the best gambits. She can use these on the man, plus very gentle fingertip friction – men's nipples easily get sore, however. If her breasts are big enough to meet, one can get a surprising degree of mutuality from intermammary intercourse. This is a good expedient on occasions when she doesn't feel like vaginal intercourse. Lay her half flat on pillows, kneel astride (big toe to her clitoris if she needs helping) and your foreskin fully retracted. Either you or she can hold the breasts together – wrap them around the shaft rather than rub the glans with them. It should protrude clear, just below her chin. An orgasm from this position, if she gets one, is "round" like a full coital orgasm, and she feels it inside. Breast orgasms from licking and handling are "in between" in feel. Rub the semen well into her breasts when you have finished (see *Semen*).

Breasts, vagina, and clitoris all at once make the fastest and most concentrated buildup of sensation once intercourse has begun, for some women at least. Few men can get a nipple orgasm, but a stiff pair of feathers is worth trying. Many easily stimulated or well-loved women can get a rather special pleasure from suckling a baby.

She says: "Men still don't understand about breasts, or are in too much of a hurry to get lower down – unlike a man's nipples, a woman's have a direct hotline to her clitoris. A man who can dial this correctly, and will only take the time, can do anything. Palm-brushing, eyelid-brushing, licking, and loud sucking like a baby can work wonders; the orgasms one gets from these are mind-blowing, without detracting a jot from intercourse to come after. Please take time."

Intercourse between the breasts is equally good in other positions – head to tail, or with her on top (especially if she has small breasts), or man sitting, woman kneeling: experiment accordingly.

breasts
One can get a surprising degree of mutuality from intermammary intercourse.

breasts

*She says "Men are in too
much of a hurry to get lower
down. Please take time."*

buttocks

Next in line after breasts, buttocks alternate with them as visual
sex stimuli for different cultures and individuals. Actually the
original primate focus, being brightly colored in most apes:
apparently equally fancied by the Mousterian culture which
produced some of the best Stone Age figurines, while more
recent tribes "made their selection by ranging their women in
a line and picking her out who projects furthest a *tergo*"
(Darwin).

   The buttocks are a major erogenous zone in both sexes, less
sensitive than breasts because they contain muscle as well as fat,
and needing stronger stimulation (holding, kneading, slapping
or even harder beating – see *Discipline*).

   Intercourse from behind (see *Rear entry, Négresse, Standing*
positions) is a pleasure in itself, but be careful if she has a weak
back. In any position, the muscular movements of coitus
stimulate the buttocks in both sexes, particularly if each holds
the partner's rear fairly tightly, one cheek in each hand. These
extra sensations are well worth cultivating deliberately. Visually,
good buttocks are a turn-on almost equally for both sexes.

buttocks
A major erogenous zone and turn-on for both sexes.

penis

More than the essential piece of male equipment, even if it is often and expressively described as a "tool", the penis has more symbolic importance than any other human organ, as a dominance signal and, by reason of having a will of its own, generally a "personality". No point in reading all this symbolism back here, except to say that lovers will experience it, and find themselves treating the penis as something very like a third party. At one moment it is a weapon or a threat, at another something they share, like a child. Without going into psychoanalysis or biology, it's not a bad test of a love-relationship that, while the penis is emphatically his, it also belongs to both of them. This particular set of programmed feelings in man is in fact the fine adjustment for all manner of experiences and feelings connected with sex-roles, identity and development. Freud's formulation, that the man is programmed to fear that the woman, or a jealous parent, will confiscate his penis, while the woman feels it is something she has lost, might be biologically true, but is over-simple. What is true is that in a good sex scene it becomes "their" penis. In any case its texture, erectility, and so on are fascinating to both sexes, and its apparent autonomy a little alarming. This is programmed, and the fact that the human penis is much bigger relatively than in other primates is probably due to these complex psychological functions: it's an esthetic as well as a functional object.

For precisely the same reasons, it collects anxieties and folklore, and is a focus for all sorts of magical manipulations. Male self-esteem and sense of identity tend to be located in it, as Samson's energy was in his hair. If it won't work, or worse, if you as a woman send it up, or down, the results will be disastrous. This explains the irrational male preoccupation with penile size. Size has absolutely nothing to do with physical serviceability in intercourse, or – since female orgasm doesn't depend on getting deeply into the pelvis – with capacity to satisfy a partner, though many women are turned on by the idea of a large one, and a few say that they feel more. The unstretched vagina is only 4 inches long anyway. If anything, thickness matters more. Nor has flaccid size anything to do with erect size – a penis which is large when at rest simply enlarges less with erection. There is no way of "enlarging" a penis. Size doesn't differ appreciably between "races", nor correlate with big muscles elsewhere. Nor, except in very rare cases, is a penis too big for a woman – the vagina will take a full-term baby. If your penis, whatever its length, hits an ovary and hurts her, don't go in so far. A woman who says she is "too small" or "too tight" is making a statement about her worries, exactly as the man who is obsessed with being too small. They need reassurance, and a different attitude to sex, not gadgets or exercises. Shape also varies – the glans can be blunt or conical. This matters only in that the conical shape can make teat-ended condoms uncomfortable through getting jammed in the teat. As to circumcision and uncircumcision, its effects are religious rather than sexual, see Foreskin. If you have anxious preconceptions, get rid of them.

Women who have really learned to enjoy sex are usually as fascinated by their lover's penis, size included, as men are by women's breasts, shape, odor, and feel, and learn to play with it fully and skillfully. Circumcised or not, it's a fascinating toy quite apart from experiencing its main use. There is a whole play scene connected with uncapping, stiffening, and handling it, making it pulsate or ejaculate, which is a major part of togetherness. This is equally important for the man – not only is it ego boosting, but also good hand- and mouthwork practically guarantee a good partner.

Care and maintenance: if you aren't circumcised, you need to retract the foreskin fully for cleaning purposes, and, if it won't retract beyond the corona all round the glans except at the front, get it seen to (this is a trifling operation with a blunt probe and doesn't necessarily mean you need circumcising). If it won't retract properly or is over-tight and gets stuck, get that seen to also. These are about the only things that are commonly wrong with a penis. Slight asymmetry often develops with time – this does no harm.

On the other hand, don't bend an erect penis, or use a position in which it could get violently bent by accident. (This usually happens with the woman on top if she is careless near orgasm, or in putting him in, and he is just short of fully stiff – keep a little control here.) It is possible, though difficult, to

penis

In a good sex scene it becomes "their" penis, not his alone.

fracture one of the two hydraulics contained in the shaft. This is very painful and can lead to pain or kinking on subsequent erection. For the same reason, avoid silly tricks with tubes, suction, or "enlarging" devices. The normal organ will stand up to extremely hard use, but not to these.

Sores, discharge, etc, are illnesses and need treatment. Even if you are both certain you are free of all sexually transmitted diseases, don't have oral intercourse with someone who has a herpes on the mouth – you can get recurrent herpes of the penis or the vulva, which is a nuisance. If the foreskin is dry from masturbation or long retraction, saliva is the best lubricant unless you have a herpes yourself. Penile cosmetics are now sold – some are deodorants, others local anesthetics to slow down response, and yet others ticklers. We don't recommend them, though see *Hairtrigger trouble*.

foreskin

Cutting off this structure is possibly the oldest human sexual ritual. It still persists – for cultural as well as supposed health reasons. Some believe that cancer of the penis and cervix is rarer when it is done (washing probably works as well) or that it slows down orgasm (for which there is no evidence). We're against it, though for some it is already too late. "To cut off the upper-most skin of the secret parts," said Dr Bulwer, "is directly against the honesty of nature, and an injurious insufferable trick put upon her." The point is that if you have a foreskin, you conserve your options. It probably doesn't make very much difference, either to masturbation or to intercourse, but it makes some, and nobody wants to lose a sensitive structure. Normally one retracts it anyway for all these purposes, but if you haven't one there is a whole range of covered-glans nuances you can't recapture. Women who have experienced both are divided – and over which looks sexier. Some find the circumcised glans "neater" and are even turned off by an unretracted prepuce as looking "feminine" (this can be an insight into the symbolic wilderness behind the original Stone Age custom), while others love the sense of discovery which goes with retraction. If you are uncircumcised and she prefers the other, retract it – if vice versa, you've had it. In function, it's probably a scent-diffusing organ – nothing to do with sensitivity.

Holding the skin back hard with the hand (her hand) during intercourse works for both circumcised and uncircumcised as an accelerator and a sensation of its own (see *Florentine*). Much of the action of various fancy penile rings is in holding back the skin of the shaft and/or the prepuce and giving extra tightness, which is why some men get extra feeling from them. If you think your glans is over-sensitive, try keeping it constantly exposed. You can always have the exposure made permanent when you've tried it. In sum, the circumcised man isn't at any important disadvantage (or advantage), but we prefer to be able to choose our egg with or without salt, and let our children do likewise.

scrotum

Basically, a control device to keep the testes at the right temperature for sperm production – moves up when you are cold and down when you are warm. It is also a highly sensitive skin area, but needs careful handling, since pressure on a testis is highly painful to its proprietor. Gentle tongue and finger work or cupping in the hand is about right. You can take it right into your mouth.

semen

There is no lovemaking without spilling this, on occasions at least. You can get it out of clothing or furnishings either with a stiff brush, when the stain has dried, or with a diluted solution of sodium bicarbonate. If you spill it over each other, massage it gently in – the pollen-odor of fresh semen is itself an aphrodisiac, which is why the smell of fresh grass or thalictrum flowers turns most people on. If you want a very copious ejaculate, he can masturbate nearly, but not quite, to orgasm about an hour beforehand to increase prostate secretion.

size

Preoccupation with the size of their genitals is as built-in biologically to men (it is a "dominance signal," like a deer's antlers) as sensitivity about their breasts and figure is to women. That, however, is its only importance. The "average" penis is about 6 inches overall when erect and about 3½ inches round, but penises come in all sizes – larger ones are spectacular, but no more effective except as visual stimuli. Smaller ones work equally well in most positions.

Accordingly, excessive preoccupation with size is an irrational anxiety, on which quacks batten – one can't increase it, any more than one can increase stature. Women should learn not to comment on it except favorably, for fear of creating a lasting hangup – men should learn not to give it a second thought. The few cases where male genitalia are really infantile occur in conjunction with major gland disturbances and are treatable but rare.

The same applies to vaginal size. No woman is too small – if she is, it is due to inability to relax, or a tough hymen. The normal vagina stretches to accommodate a full-term baby – and a tight woman gives the man extra intense feelings. Nor is any vagina too large: if it seems a loose fit, switch to a posture in which her thighs are pressed together. Genital anatomy probably fixes which postures work best for a given couple, but no more than that. With rare exceptions, men and women are universally adapted.

Non-erect size in the male is equally unimportant – some men before erection show no penile shaft at all, but extend to full size easily. The same applies to testicle weight – it varies, as does nose or mouth size, but has little to do with function. Small genitals are usually due to active muscles in the under-skin layer – a cold bath will shrink the best endowed male down to Greek statue proportions. The only practical exception is that with a very big penis, and a very small woman, she should be careful on top, or she will knock an ovary (which feels as a man feels if he knocks a testicle), and he shouldn't thrust too hard until he knows he won't hurt her. As to the size of other structures, such as breasts, these may be individual turn-ons, but every build has its sexual opportunities built-in: use them.

skin

Skin is our chief extragenital sexual organ – underrated by men, who concentrate on the penis and clitoris; better understood by women.

She says: "The smell and feel of a man's skin probably has more to do with sexual attraction (or the opposite) than any other single feature, even though you may not be conscious of it."

Skin stimulation is a major component of all sex. Not only its feel when touched, but also its coolness, texture and tightness are triggers for a whole range of sex feelings. These can be boosted in some people by emphasis, and by adding other textures, especially fur, rubber, leather, or tight clothing. Much underrated part of human sexual response, to be played to the full if it turns you on. See *Clothes, Friction rub, Pattes d'araignée, Tongue bath*. Use these to educate your own and your partner's skin.

lubrication

The best sexual lubricant is saliva. For most sexual purposes, greasy materials, such as petroleum jelly, are too greasy and being unwettable they leave an unpleasant feel. Jellies tend to cut sensation too much. The normal, excited vagina is correctly set for friction; if she is too wet, as may happen on the Pill, dry gently with a handkerchief-wrapped finger (not tissues – you'll never stop finding the bits). To increase friction, try honey – it washes off easily and is harmless. Interference with friction is the main drawback of contraceptive creams, foams, and so on, making them unpopular with some couples, but see *AIDS & other sexually transmitted diseases*.

earlobes

Underrated erogenous zone, together with the adjacent neck skin – the small area behind the ear has a hotline to the visceral nerves via the vagus – and the nape of the neck. As with all extragenital sites, they are more effective in women than men. Once established (gentle fingering, sucking, etc, during build-up and before orgasm, to condition the response), earlobes can trigger full climax from manipulation alone. Some women find the noise of heavy breathing excruciating and a definite turn-off, so be careful.

Heavy earrings help, and can actually maintain subliminal erotic excitement, especially if long enough to brush the neck when she turns her head – this is the original function of the large Eastern and Spanish candelabra-type earrings. The sex difference in response probably accounts for their relative rarity worldwide in male fashions.

Swinging weights as erotic stimuli to condition a particular area aren't confined to the ears. Skillful handling of other types of body jewelry can provide additional erotic pleasure.

navel

Fascinating to lovers, like all the details of the human body. It's not only decorative, but has a lot of cultivable sexual sensation as well; it fits the finger, tongue, glans or big toe, and merits careful attention when you kiss or touch. Intercourse in the navel is practicable (there are stories of naive couples who thought that was the usual way, and it's a common childhood fantasy about how sex is conducted). If she is plump, she can hold up the skin on each side to make labia. In any case, the finger or tongue tip slip into it naturally in both sexes.

armpit

Classical site for kisses. Should on no account be shaved (see *Cassolette*). Can be used instead of the palm to silence your partner at climax – if you use your palm, rub it over your own and your partner's armpit area first.

Axillary intercourse is an occasional variation. Handle it as for intermammary intercourse (see *Breasts*) but with your penis under her right arm – well under, so that friction is on the shaft, not the glans, as in any other unlubricated area. Put her left arm round your neck, and hold her right hand behind her with your right hand. She will get her sensations from the pressure against her breasts, helped by your big toe pressed to her clitoris if she wants it. Not an outstandingly rewarding trick, but worth trying if you like the idea.

earlobes
Dramatic results are obtainable, but not with heavy breathing!

skin

Its importance as a sex organ is grossly underrated by men; women not only understand it better but rate it much higher.

navel
To kiss or touch with, even,
possibilities of intercourse.

feet

Very attractive sexually to some people – he can get an orgasm, if wished, between her soles.

Their erotic sensitivity varies a lot. Sometimes, when they're the only part you can reach, they serve as channels of communication, and the big toe is a good penis substitute.

Tickling the soles excites some people out of their minds; for others it's agony, but increases general arousal. You can try it as a stimulus or, briefly, for testing bondage. Firm pressure on the sole at the instep, however administered, is erogenic to most people. But so can almost any touch be in a woman who's that way minded – one can get a full orgasm from a foot, a finger, or an earlobe. Men respond less far but equally easily if the handling is skillful.

armpit
*A classical site for
perfumed kisses.*

big toe

The pad of the male big toe applied to the clitoris or the vulva generally is a magnificent erotic instrument. The famous gentleman in erotic prints who is keeping six women occupied is using tongue, penis, both hands, and both big toes. Use the toe in mammary or armpit intercourse or any time you are astride her, or sit facing as she lies or sits. Make sure the nail isn't sharp. In a restaurant, one can surreptitiously remove a shoe and sock, reach over, and keep her in almost continuous orgasm with all four hands fully in view on the table top and no sign of contact – a party trick which rates as really advanced sex, though she may appear more than a little distracted. She has less scope, but can learn to masturbate him with her two big toes. The toes are definitely erogenic areas and can be kissed, sucked, tickled, or tied with stimulating results.

hair

Head hair has a lot of Freudian overtones – in ancient mythology, it's a sign of virility, witness Samson or Hercules, and some of these associations persist.

Our culture, having learned in previous generations to associate long hair with women and short hair with manly

conformity, has been occasionally excited to frenzy when young males rejected the stereotype, and wore their hair, in the words of the seventeenth-century Harvard MS "in the manner of ruffians and barbarous Indians" – or of George Washington.

Freud thought that long female hair acted as reassurance to the male by being a substitute for the phallus women don't have. Be that as it may, long male hair today tends to go with a less anxious idea of maleness.

Sex play with long hair is great because of its texture – you can handle it, touch each other with it, and generally use it as one more resource. Some women are turned on by a fair amount of masculine body hair because it looks virile, others are turned off by it because it looks animal – this seems to be a matter of attitude.

Male face hair is another focus of convention – sometimes everyone has it as a social necessity or a response to convention, at other times it is persecuted, or confined to sailors, pioneers, and creative people such as artists and chefs. Schopenhauer thought that it covered the parts of the face "which express the moral feelings," and disapproved on the grounds that it was immodest to wear a sex signal in the middle of one's face. Today you can please yourself, or better, your partner.

big toe
A sexual organ of considerable versatility, yielding great pleasure.

pubic hair

Shave it off if you prefer: we don't, but some people do. If you do shave it once, you're committed to a prickly interregnum while it regrows. Some prefer it off in the interest of total nudity or prefer the hardness of the bare pubis – most find it decorative. Most lovers regard pubic hair as a resource. Try brushing it lightly and learn to caress with it.

It can be combed, twirled, kissed, held, even pulled. In the woman it can move the whole pubis, skillfully handled, to the point of orgasm. For the woman, it's often best not to shave, but to trim, confining the triangle to the middle of the pubis with a bare strip each side – the pattern of youth – removing hair which comes outside a g-string or swimsuit, and trimming enough to make the vulva fully visible. Better not try to dye it to match head hair – it never looks right – still less to bleach it. It is a myth that you can tell whether a blonde is natural from the colour of her pubic hair. It is often shades darker than head hair – in black-haired women, it can be nearly blue. Men can shave if they like, or if their partners like, but it's difficult to shave the scrotum. Don't use depilatories around the genitals – they can burn. You may need to shave the penile shaft and root to use condoms – otherwise the hairs can get caught. This can produce sharp pain at a time when you should be experiencing intense pleasure.

pubic hair
*Most lovers regard it as
an additional resource, not
an embarrassment to be
shaved off.*

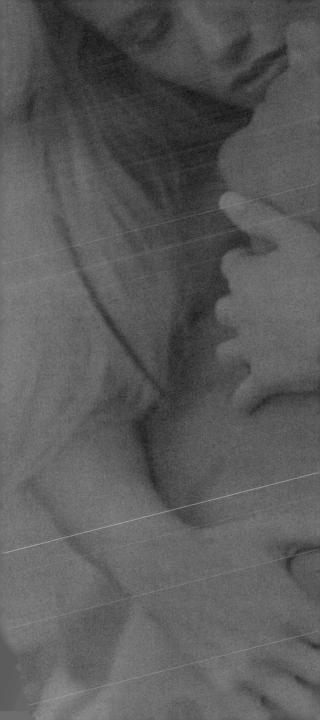

appetizers

real sex
Tenderness, touching and being together are as much "real sex" as vaginal intercourse.

real sex

The sort our culture and most mass media propaganda don't recognize: not that intercourse, or masturbation, or genital kisses aren't real sex, but some other things are real sex too, which people need, but which don't excite our time and age. We can list some: being together in a situation of pleasure, or of danger, or just of rest (if we admitted these as sexual we'd run the risk of having to love other people as people, and that would be worrying or inconvenient, to us or society); touching; old-fashioned expedients like holding hands (permissiveness makes more orgasms, but we miss out on the pleasures of old-fashioned dating, kisses, and looks that vagina-obsessed males think of as schmalz); sleeping together even without, or especially after, intercourse.

Most women don't need telling this, but are as shy about telling it to males, for fear of seeming sentimental, as males are about object-preferences or aggressive needs. Don't get stuck with the view that only those things which Auntie calls sexual are sexual. In a book on sexual elaboration, this needs saying, if you are concerned with love rather than an Olympic pentathlon. People in our culture who are hung up on the Olympic bit don't get much from it unless it helps them to learn this.

food

Dinner is a traditional preface to sex. In old-time France or Austria, one booked a restaurant room with no handle on the outside of the door. At the same time, there is a French saying that love and digestion went to bed together, and the offspring was apoplexy. This isn't quite true. On the other hand, immediately after a heavy meal is not an ideal moment – you can easily make your partner, especially the woman if she's underneath, sick.

A meal can be an erotic experience in itself – for a demonstration of how a woman can excite a man by eating a chickenleg or a pear "at" him, cannibal-style, see the lovely burlesque in the 1963 film of *Tom Jones* or the outrageously sensuous equivalents in *Tampopo* and *9½ Weeks*.

A meal *à deux* is, quite certainly, a direct lead-in to love play (see *Big toe, Remote control*), but don't include alcohol. Recent work shows that even in small doses it's a powerful neutering drug, and it's quite the most common cause of unexpected impotence – so forget the folklore and ignore the commercials. If you're serious about sex, stay with mineral water. Love and food mixed well in Greek and Roman times when you reclined together on a couch, or fed one another (geishas do this still). Some people enjoy food-and-sex games (custard or ice-cream on the skin, grapes in the pussy, and so on), which are great for regressive orality, but messy for an ordinary domestic setting. Most lovers with privacy like to eat naked together and take it from there according to taste.

History is littered with "aphrodisiac" foods – these are magic (eryngo roots, which look like testicles, phallic asparagus, and so on), olfactory (fish, tomatoes straight off the plant, which smell sexy), or miscellaneous. One can't prove that onions, eels – phallic and otherwise – ginseng root, and so on don't work on some people. The trouble is that any reputed aphrodisiac works if you think it will, while many true pharmacological responses can get overridden in particular individuals by other factors. Broad beans are a reputed aphrodisiac – not only do they look like testicles, but they also contain dopamine. We both respond so quickly to one another that any effect of this sort is hard to gauge personally. Hot spices, which induce skin flushing, are another physiologically plausible line of attack.

But no alleged aphrodisiac is a lifesaver or comes up to the combined effect of "the time and the place and the loved one together". However, experiment by all means. Only very heavy meals and excessive drinking are specific turn-offs, and therefore to be avoided.

dancing

All dancing in pairs looks toward intercourse. In this respect, the Puritans were dead right. The development of no-contact dances has come about because one doesn't now need a social excuse to embrace, but as an excitant it need not involve contact at all – in fact, most dancing today is far more erotic than a clinch because you aren't too close to see one another. At its best, this sort of dance is simply intercourse by remote control (see *Remote control*).

Most good lovers dance well together. They can do it publicly or in private, clothed or naked. Stripping one another while dancing is a sensation on its own. Don't hurry to full intercourse – dance until his erection is unbearable and she is almost coming, brought there by rhythm and the sight and perfume of each other alone. Even then you need not stop.

Most couples can insert and continue dancing, either in each other's arms, or limbo-style, linked only by the penis, provided they are the right heights. Unfortunately, this means that the woman needs to be at least as tall as the man, while as a rule she's going to be shorter. Otherwise he has to bend his knees, which is tiring. If you can't dance inserted, and if she is small, pick her up into one of the Hindu standing positions, legs round waist, arms round neck, and continue like this. If she is too heavy to pick up, turn her and take her stooping from behind, still keeping the dance going.

Seduction, or encouragement, while dancing is a natural. In the days of formal dancing, one used to wish that the woman had her breasts on her back, where one could reach them, but that would have made it too easy. Gentle pressure, rhythm, sight and scent, and a knowledge of remote-control methods are all that is needed to bring the dance on to its erotic conclusion.

dancing
*At its best, dancing is
simply intercourse by
remote control.*

exercises

The Viennese Turnergesellschaft professors tried to make sex into a form of physical training. Good general tone certainly helps, but it's equally true that sexual exercise tones you up better than jogging.

Adolescent masturbation, if it's guiltless and enjoyed, is one of the best specifically sexual exercises, and the man can use it at any age in learning to slow down his response to a level which gives the woman a chance. She, for her part, can learn to use her vaginal and pelvic muscles (see *Pompoir*) "by throwing her mind into the part concerned," says Richard Burton. This superlative knack can be learned because, traditionally, women in South India learned it. How exactly they learn has never been written down, unfortunately, and the first person to teach this properly to women who don't have the knack naturally will make a fortune. Whether the commercial device with a rubber cylinder and a pressure-gauge helps we simply don't know,

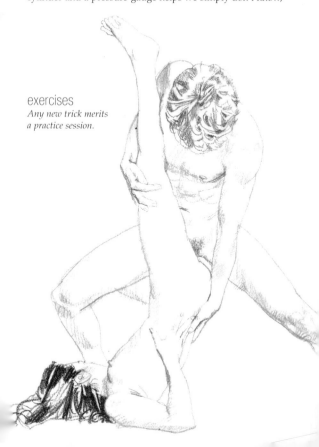

exercises
*Any new trick merits
a practice session.*

since our female half has the trick naturally. The technique to try would involve having a bulb in the vagina and a light or pressure gauge to enable you to know when you were doing the right thing. Anyone can learn to waggle his ears in any direction in 30 minutes flat if he watches the ear on closed-circuit TV. This makes us think that the commercial gadget is well worth trying. If she "throws her mind" with him in situ she should master it, and he can tell her when she is succeeding. Once learned, it is wholly involuntary and needs no effort.

What we do suggest is that for any new trick you arrange a practice session in anticipation. The time to learn new figures isn't on the ice rink or dance floor. The most common reason that an elaboration you both wanted disappoints, whether it's a fancy posture or some dodge such as bondage, which needs to be quickly and efficiently set up, is the attempt to use it in actual, excited lovemaking "from cold" – so that you mess about, lose the thread, and wish you hadn't bothered with it or blame whoever suggested it. The usual and regrettable outcome is never to try again.

Not that rehearsal need be cold-blooded or taken out of actual lovemaking. Anticipation being good in itself, you first fantasize about it, sit down together, plan, and rehearse. Then fit the actual trial-for-size into the waiting periods between bouts – when you're both excited enough not to feel silly, but not ready to go completely: try it while waiting for the next erection. Remember even the most accomplished musician has to practice, though in love once learned is never forgotten. If it works first time, you should get the erection – in that case, go where it takes you. This means you can rehearse something new for each special occasion, mastering every movement, but quite deliberately holding back and not playing it live until the appointed time. The waiting will help when that arrives.

To practice things you must try in full erection, make the effort and try the new posture when you have one – either without movement, if you are set on waiting till later, or switching after a few strokes to something else. Of course, if it takes over, as it may, you might as well carry on, and turn practice into performance there and then. For most postures, you can try wearing g-strings, so as to get the motions without actual contact, and some people find this exciting in itself.

clothed intercourse
*If it's not reliable as a
contraceptive method, it
doesn't fit the needs of
safe sex either.*

clothed intercourse

Really a heavy-petting technique: she keeps her panties or g-string on, he carries out all the movements of straight intercourse as far as the cloth will allow. Favorite ethnologic variant, chiefly for premarital intercourse – called *badana* in Turkey, *metsha* in Xhosa, etc. Odd we have no special word.

Not reliable as a contraceptive unless the ejaculation position is fully interfemoral, i.e. with the glans well clear of the vulva, cloth or no cloth. Some people who used this before marriage like to go back to it either as a starter, or during menstrual periods. Inclined to be "dry" and make the man sore if it goes on too long – many women can get a fair orgasm from it.

femoral intercourse

Another dodge, like clothed intercourse, to preserve virginity,
avoid pregnancy etc, in cultures which cared about virginity
and had no contraceptives. Comes for us under the heading of
substitutes. Used from before or behind, or in any other posture
where she can press her thighs together. The penis goes between
them, with the shaft between her labia, but the glans well clear
of the vagina, and she presses hard. Gives the woman a special
set of sensations – sometimes keener than on penetration, so
worth trying. One need not be so rigid about technique as were
our forefathers, who had to try to keep sperm out of the vulva
at any cost. With care one can do this from behind with the
glans actually on the clitoris, with striking results. Good
menstrual variant, or for at least a few strokes before you go in
as usual.

kisses

These, at one level, don't require teaching, but it's easy to be so
set on insertion that one overlooks them (see *Real sex*). Lip and
tongue kisses add immensely to intercourse in all face-to-face
positions; breast kisses are essential if the woman isn't to miss a
whole range of feeling; genital kisses (see *Mouth music*) are a
tender resource on their own. Kisses can be put anywhere on
the body, they can be given with lips, tongue, penis, labia, or
eyelashes – mouth kisses range from a mere touch to the kiss *à
la cannibale*, which leaves a bruise.

A lot of people maintain mouth contact continuously
throughout intercourse, and prefer face-to-face positions for this
reason. The deep tongue kiss can either be a second penetration,
the man's tongue imitating exactly the rhythm of what is going
on elsewhere, or she can give it, penetrating him, to call the
rhythm. Even without any penetration, some people favor a
tongue-battle which can last minutes or even hours, bringing
several orgasms for the woman; this form of non-genital heavy
petting is called *maraîchignage*. If you are in private, move on to
breasts, and go from there.

Another pleasure is to make her a carpet of flowers, by
covering every inch of her body with small, close kisses: then
she can reply, using lipstick to mark where she's been. From
there, it is only a little way to doing the same with a tongue-tip
(see *Tongue bath*): moreover, unlike a man, she has two mouths
to kiss with, and some women use them beautifully. Eyelids,
too, can be used for nipple, lip, glans, and skin kisses.

If you haven't at least kissed her mouth, shoulders, neck,
breasts, armpits, fingers, palms, toes, soles, navel, genitals, and
earlobes, you haven't really kissed her: it is no trouble to fill in
the gaps for completeness and makes a touching compliment.

A good mouth kiss should leave its recipient breathless but
not asphyxiated (leave an airway open), and nobody likes their

kisses
He has only one mouth – she
has two.

kisses
*Move on to make her a carpet
of flowers by covering her body
with close kisses.*

nose squashed into their face. Clean your teeth before making love, and, if you are having whisky, garlic etc., both of you have it.

handwork

Sex for all males and many females begins in the handwork class – both when we start to discover our own bodies, and when we start to have access to each other's. For both sexes, it is basic training – in mutual sex, good handwork is never superseded. A couple who can masturbate each other really skillfully can do anything else they like, and a generation which has been brought up to masturbate with enjoyment from pre-adolescence will have a flying start in forming some sensual attitudes. Handwork is not a "substitute" for vaginal intercourse, but something quite different, giving a different type of orgasm, and the orgasm one induces oneself is different again from orgasm induced by a partner. In full intercourse, it is a preparation – to stiffen the man, or to give the woman one or more preliminary peaks before insertion. After intercourse, it is the natural lead-in to a further round. Moreover, most men can get a second orgasm sooner from partner stimulation than from the vagina, and a third after that if they masturbate themselves.

A woman who has the divine gift of lechery and loves her partner will masturbate him well, and a woman who knows how to masturbate a man - subtly, unhurriedly, and mercilessly – will almost always make a superlative partner. She needs intuitive empathy and real enjoyment of a penis, holding it in just the right place, with just the right amount of pressure and movement, and timing her action in bursts to coincide with his feeling - stopping or slowing to keep him in suspense, speeding up to control his climax. Some men can't stand really proficient masturbation to climax unless they are securely tied (see *Bondage*) and virtually none can hold still for slow masturbation.

The variation can be endless, even if she hasn't the choice of foreskin back, foreskin not back, which again yield two quite distinct nuances. If he isn't circumcised, she will probably need to avoid rubbing the glans itself, except in pursuit of very special effects. Her best grip is just below the groove, with the skin back as far as it will go, and using two hands – one pressing hard near the root, holding the penis steady, or fondling the scrotum, the other making a thumb-and-first finger ring, or a whole hand grip. She should vary this and, in prolonged masturbation, change hands often. For a full orgasm, she sits comfortably on his chest or kneels astride him. During every extended sexual session, one orgasm – usually the second or third – is well worth giving in this way: the French professionals who used no other method and called themselves *"les filles de la veuve Poignet"* didn't only stay in business through fear of infection. It is well worth devoting time to perfecting this technique – it fully expresses love, and can be domesticated in any bedroom.

Rolling the penis like pastry between the palms of two hands is another technique, best used for producing an erection rather than going for orgasm. Firm pressure with one finger at the midpoint between penis and anus is another. For some occasions, she can try to copy his own favorite method of self-masturbation. When she uses her own rhythm it can have a different and sometimes more startling effect.

He needs to notice how she masturbates herself. Most men neglect the labia in favor of the clitoris. Clitoral rubbing can be as mind-blowing for her as slow masturbation is for him, but it can be painful if it is unskillful, repeated too often, or straight after an orgasm achieved in this way. She says: "The main difficulty from the man's point of view is that the ideal pressure point varies from hour to hour so he should allow her to guide him to the right place. Most men think they know automatically, having succeeded once – they are often wrong."

For preparation as well as orgasm, the flat of the hand on the vulva with the middle finger between the lips, and its tip moving in and out of the vagina, while the ball of the palm presses hard just above the pubis, is probably the best method. Steady rhythm is the most important thing, taking it from her hip movements, and alternating with gentle lip stretching – then a full attack on the clitoris and its hood with the forefinger or little finger, thumb deeply in the vagina (keep your nails short). For faster response, hold her open with one hand and work gently with all the fingers of the other (in this case she may need to be fixed down). Switch to the tongue occasionally if she becomes dry, because she won't realize until afterwards how sore you have made her.

In mutual masturbation to orgasm, you take out your need to move on your partner. It works better than sixty-nine because under these circumstances you can let go without losing your partner or hurting them. Side by side on your backs is probably the best position.

However much sex you have, you will still need simple, own-hand masturbation – not only during periods of separation, but also simply when you feel like another orgasm. Some women feel left out if they find their partner masturbating; however, if you feel vibrations when he thinks you are asleep and want to get in on the act, tackle him there and then, and finish him yourself at full speed or, better, start on him slow-style then stop, tie him, and make him watch you masturbate yourself, slowly and with style, before you put him out of his misery. The unexpected sight of a woman giving herself an orgasm when he cannot move is unbearably exciting for most men. Make sure he can't get loose. Finally, watching each other take the last orgasm separately but together makes a wonderful end to any afternoon in bed.

handwork
*The variations of grip, rhythm
and pace are endless.*

pattes d'araignée
*Erotic massage at its
most delicate.*

pattes d'araignée

Pattes d'araignée, literally "spider's legs", is tickling erotic massage, using the pulps of the fingers, with the lightest possible touch, aiming to stimulate not so much the skin as the almost invisible skin hairs: not on the genitals, but all the next most sensitive places – nipples and around, neck, chest, belly, insides of arms and thighs, armpits, hollow of the back, soles and palms, scrotum, space between it, and the anus. Use both hands; keep a steady progression of movement going with one, and make surprise attacks with the other.

The whole essence is in the extreme lightness of the touch – more electric than tickling. Feathers, bristlegloves, or vibrators give a quite different sensation. If you are agile, don't forget you have toes as well as fingers, and hair in various places, including eyelids, to vary the sensation. A set of finger-cots with textures from cardcloth to mink is easy to use; the real and original French style with fingertips is difficult to learn, but unforgettable by either sex. It's one of the two general skin stimulants (the other is the *Tongue bath*) which work even on not very skin-conscious males.

friction rub

The original meaning of shampoo, which is gentle kneading massage all over. Much more pleasant if you rub each other all over with massage oil. Sit on something that doesn't matter, and rub each other, together or in turns – moisturizer or soap lather work well if you haven't got a special preparation.

This always ends in genital handwork, then intercourse, then bath together. Semen would be the ideal medium, but it is too little and too late – bottled lotion is a substitute for this particular fantasy. She kneads his muscles, with fingers and a vibrator as well if they like; he concentrates on her breasts, buttocks, loins, and neck. With practice, these sensations are well worth cultivating. Massage parlors may get busted regularly, but they have nothing one can't do at home   apart from the fact that they are male-orientated, not mutual, and lay on a whole troupe of women for every man.

feathers

Recommended by some for skin stimulation (breasts, body surface generally, more than the actual genitals and palms and soles). Try stiff wiry ones (heron or egret) or an old-fashioned feather duster.

feathers
A stimulating alternative when tongues tire.

tongue bath

Going systematically over every square inch of a partner, tied if they like, with long, slow, broad tongue strokes. Start behind, turn them, and cover the front surface after, so as to be in position to go on to coition or hand- and mouthwork. If the woman gives this, she follows it by covering the whole available surface equally systematically with slow strokes of her open vulva. Mini versions cover particular areas in the same way.

tongue bath
Slow, all-over arousal.

blowing

Not the slang sense (see *Mouth music*) but quite simply making a current of air on the (preferably pre-wetted) skin of any part of the body, either from the lips or from a hairdryer with the heat turned off. The best way to moisten an erogenous area is with the tongue, though for more extensive operations one can obviously use water or lotion. Air on a wet sensitive surface produces a sensation which can drive some people of either sex out of their minds – experiment on a small scale, using your natural equipment (saliva and breath). In the case of earlobes, breathe in, not out, or you'll deafen your partner. Elsewhere, use steady, continuous exhalation with the lips about an inch from the skin. The natural sequel to a tongue bath. For a bigger operation, use the hairdryer – the result is far wilder than the conventional routine with feathers, except for palms and soles. Try mixing the two by hitching a couple of feathers to the dryer nozzle on threads. Never (see *Hazards*) use a strong air source, and never blow into the vagina or any other body orifice (except the mouth).

blowing
A mind-blowing sensation on skin that has been tongue-bathed.

bites

Hindu eroticians classified these at huge length. Gentle nibbling (of the penis, breasts, skin, fingers, ears, labia, clitoris, armpit hair) is part of the general excitatory repertoire. Hard bites at the moment of orgasm excite some people, but for most, like other painful stimuli, they are a turn-off. Women tend to bite more often than men, perhaps because they enjoy being bitten more than men do. (Remember that often your partner will do to you what they really want done to them – being aware of this is the great secret of communicating sex.) Love-bruises, on the neck and elsewhere, which some lovers find act like a constant playback, setting off more lovemaking every time they are seen, aren't made by biting, but by strong, continuous suction kisses. Sharp nips to the skin aren't as a rule erotic.

Be careful of biting at or near orgasm – the jaws go into spasm and you can bite really hard – in fact don't have an orgasm deliberately with a breast, penis, or finger in your mouth. The need to bite can be taken out on something neutral like cloth or hair. This seems to be a case where the mammalian program of reflexes is over-tough for human enjoyment.

fighting

The occasional fights, often physical, which all lovers have would have nothing to do with sex if some couples weren't directly excited by them, often without knowing it. That real anger has erotic effects is a matter of true folklore. The French have a song which goes:

Hey, Mister Copper,
Colin's beating up his mistress:
Mister Copper, let them get on with it –
It will end with kisses.

Or, as one woman put it, "We found the old tenderness routine wasn't enough: he likes to use violence and it excites me to resist him. I find the pain exciting, but he's started to hurt me in other contexts and I'm afraid how far it will go." The trouble is that, as we've several times remarked, our image of love is uptight about the very real elements of aggression in normal sexuality – which makes us prone to mix erotic violence with real spite or real anger, and confuse two quite distinct things, the quarrel which lets off steam, or is an appeal for help, and sexual stimulation. We aren't talking here about borderline sadists. There are women who unconsciously want some aggression (and have timid partners) who needle the man into a fight without knowing why. The mixture is a bad one, and usually goes sour.

To need some degree of violence in sex, rather than the glutinous unphysical kind of love which the tradition propagates, is statistically pretty normal. But the way to meet this need isn't to use rows to fuel it, but rather to learn the purposive uses of play. True, the over-gentle spouse is likely to be blocked about aggression, and nonplussed by a demand "now try to rape me." He's been taught not to treat women like that – if he's excessively over-gentle, he may be sitting on a strong need to do so. But if these things can once be talked about, you can make him (or her) learn the uses of sexual play – which is why we've included some pretty rough-looking games by marriage guidance standards – and this without the need to mix them up with real day-to-day angers and frustrations which can get out of hand, especially with the wrong partner. If he's over-gentle, don't needle him, teach him.

With a normal partner, don't be ashamed if you really fight (most people do), but don't treat it as a kick or a way of turning on a partner's aggression. Use play, and keep it in the sexual situation. Cultivate pillow talk to unblock fantasies – ask each other just short of orgasm, "What would you like to do to me, like me to do to you, now?" – "now" meaning at the fantasy level. See *Birdsong at morning*.

Also, as nearly always with man, symbolisms are generally bigger kicks than over-literal enactments. But some couples get a lot of fun out of extended struggles, premeditated or impromptu ("love wrestling" in the old Viennese athletic tradition). Enthusiasts go in for elaborate handicaps: time limits, no-biting-or-scratching, and so on. Most people find fairly robust but reasonable tussling quite enough, others play elaborate finding-fault-and-spanking games (don't play these over real faults). Women who enjoy an extra sensation of violence and/or helplessness differ whether they feel this more held down or tied up: men can take out quite a lot of the violence component in the actual process of penetration and working for orgasm. Once understood, none of this range of needs is scary, and can be stopped spilling out of sex into cruelty or the normal resentments felt by any two people who live together. Actually, it tends to discharge these.

Nothing we've said excludes the tenderness of sex. If you haven't learned that sexual violence can be tender and

bites
Hard biting turns most people off, but gentle nibbling is a powerful excitant.

tenderness violent, you haven't begun to play as real lovers, unless you are people (and there are such) whose tenderness is absolutely unalloyed: these needn't worry about the risks of fighting. See *Bondage*, *Discipline*.

If you do have a real fight, make sure to end it in bed. At least it's the best way to finish. Don't ever put up with real violence – it will escalate, however much the aggressor apologizes. Real, spiteful violence from a partner is a common cause of death or injury in women. Don't put up with it, and don't give second chances – leave, or go to the police. Sadistic bullies are incurable by love.

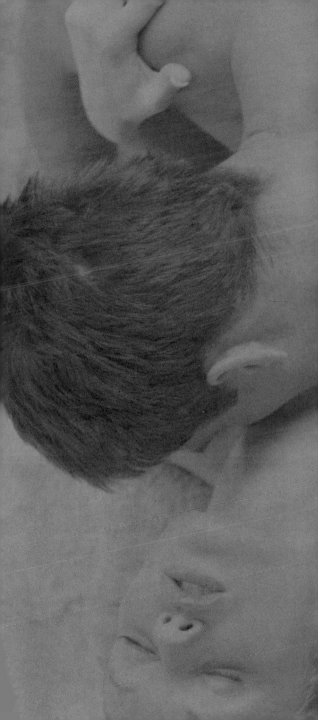

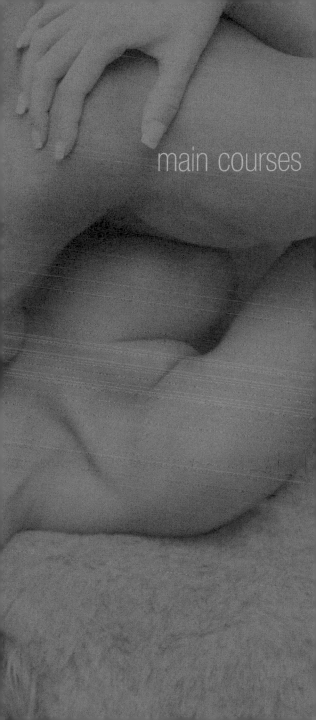

main courses

postures

Endless time has been spent throughout history, chiefly by nonplaying coaches, in describing and giving fancy names to upwards of 600 of these – collecting them is obviously a human classificatory hobby. Most of the non-extreme postures come naturally, and few of the extreme ones merit more than a single visit out of curiosity. The only part we regret is the loss of the fancy names, Arabic, Sanskrit, or Chinese, which they have been given across cultures and down the centuries.

Most people now know the obvious ones and have learned which make for quick and slow orgasm and how to use them in series. A few people, either for symbolic or anatomical reasons, can only get orgasm in one or two.

Inspection will indicate which fit special situations such as pregnancy, fat male with thin female, height differences, etc. Only trial will indicate which work best, or at all, orgasm-wise. Couples often start by trying the lot, but nearly inevitably end up with one or two, going back to the book for special occasions.

Some of the really wild fantasies in oriental manuscripts do have a point – the woman astride in Mughal pictures who is balancing lighted lamps on her hands, head, and shoulders or shooting at a target with a bow is only showing that she can bring the man off with her vaginal muscles alone while keeping the rest of her still (see *Pompoir*). Others are mystical or merely gymnastic. All the poses we show are practicable (we've tried them for fit, if not to orgasm) and more or less rewarding according to inclination.

mouth music

In the first half of the twentieth century, genital kisses, or rather the taboos on them, were a king pretext for divorce on grounds of perversity, cruelty, etc. We've come some way since then – now there are textbooks, and they figure in movies. Personal preferences and unpreferences apart, most people now know that they are one of the best things in sexual intimacy. In regard to AIDS, the omnipresent preoccupation, there seems to be no clearcut case of its being transmitted by oral sex, but if you don't know your partner it must be wise to avoid it – in particular to avoid contact with semen.

Soixante-neuf is fine, but has some drawbacks. It needs attention and care to give your partner your best, and consequently you can't go berserk over it, as you can over a mutual genital orgasm: impending orgasm, especially in the woman, just isn't compatible with careful technique, and the man can even be bitten. Another slight but, for some men, real defect is that in *soixante-neuf* the woman is the wrong way round for tongue work on the most sensitive surface of the glans (this explains the acrobatics in some Indian temple statues, which aim to get both mutuality and a better approach for the

postures

The variety of possible ways of having intercourse is an ancient fascination, the pleasure of trying them a renewable inspiration.

woman). Our own experience is that mutual genital kisses are wonderful, but if you are going to orgasm it's usually better to take turns.

Who goes first is clearly a matter of preference, but one can give the woman dozens of purely preliminary orgasms in this way, as many as she can take, and she will still want to go on from there, so the man had better save himself for later. A few men can't take even the shortest genital kiss before ejaculating – these should save it until they need a new erection, when it is a uniquely effective way of raising the dead.

Some women do and some don't like the man to go all the way and ejaculate (if they love him very much, that may make all the difference, but not always). Those who don't can easily stop just short of getting him there, shift to another foyer (between the breasts, for example), or they can compress with both hands to gain time – this needs alertness and doesn't always work. It's also apt to wreck his orgasm. Others once they are used to it don't find the experience complete unless their lover does ejaculate. John Hunter wrote, "The semen would appear both by smell and taste to be a mawkish kind of substance: but when held in the mouth it produced a warmth similar to spices." If the slight bitterness, rather than the whole idea, is what they dislike, it can easily be avoided by taking him really deeply. With experienced women we guess it is about fifty-fifty, come or not come; in any

postures
Most of the non-extreme postures come naturally.

case, you can always ask, and partners soon learn each other's
tastes. She says: "A couple of important points to remember here
are that retching is a reflex action if something large is poked
down your throat; so, if she does retch it may well not be because
she hates it, but because she can't help herself. A large penis will
also stretch the mouth quite a lot, and, if she is covering her teeth
with her lips to protect you, violent movements may lacerate
them. Be considerate."

Normal genital odor is a big part of the genital kiss for both
partners, which means that the parties should wash often, but
not immediately beforehand: they ought to know each other
well enough to say, if it is ever disagreeable, and switch or wait.
A few minutes' vigorous intercourse will often put this right,
though the woman's odor changes in character. Contraceptives
can upset it too. The marketers of intimate deodorants and
flavored vaginal douches show evidence only of sexual
inexperience – nobody wants peach sauce on, say, scampi.
Seaweed odors or musk would be more in key. Many women
are unaware of the extent to which their cassolettes are their
secret weapon. Some men respond violently to it without
realizing the fact; it's also the ideal perfume fixative, and a
touch behind the ears at a dance, in advance of, or instead of,
bottle perfume can be deadly. His, by contrast, will please her
more the longer she loves him. Wash with white soap, and here

mouth music

A spontaneous genital kiss to a man is one of the most moving gestures in the whole sexual experience.

as everywhere treat deodorants the way a chef would treat deflavorants. How the hippie generation thought you could live the good sex life without washing defeats explanation.

For some couples, the simultaneous, 69-type kiss really does represent the ultimate in sensation. For them, since loss of control will be complete, the woman can't be the berserk type, nor want him to stop short of ejaculating. The woman-on-top position in most books is all right, especially if she combines mouth with handwork, but it gives the man a stiff neck. We favor the no-cushions position, i.e. head to tail on their sides, each with the under thigh drawn up as a cushion for the partner's head. The man can open her widely by slipping his arm in the crook of her upper knee.

The mutual kiss can be long or short; the short is just in passing – the long can last minutes or hours according to taste and speed. Both fit nicely between rounds of intercourse, as well as acting as hors d'oeuvres or a corpse reviver.

If, on the other hand, they are going alternately, let him start, preferably in this same no-cushions position, while she does very little. Then it can be her turn; or they can go on to intercourse, putting off fellatio until he has had one orgasm and a rest and is due for his next erection. In this way, she can abandon herself, and watch her technique when she sucks him. She will probably get the best results with what the Chinese call the "jade flute" position – an instrument which is self-explanatory, and is played like a recorder, facing him, thumbs underneath, fingers on top. Her technique depends on her man – for instance, on whether or not he is circumcised. Not all men find tongue or lip contact with the glans pleasurable. For some it's ecstasy, while others prefer foreskin movement over the covered glans with the shaft held tight. The various sorts of nibbling, etc., described in sex books come naturally to most people. One finds them out on a basis of learn and teach. For a more active male position and a fast orgasm, she lies back, and he has oral coitus as fully and deeply as she can stand it. She must keep her teeth well open, making him a vagina with her lips and tongue. He needs to keep a little control, to avoid being involuntarily bitten.

The reverse equivalent is when she kneels astride and gives herself, exactly as in a passionate mouth-to-mouth kiss, brushing first, then open and deeply, while he uses long tongue strokes from the vagina to the clitoris, with an extra twitch to her glans as he reaches it each time.

When it's his initiative, he can do worse than try the cascade position, if she is portable. This is really only 69 standing up, but it gives her the unique sensation of an orgasm head-downward. To get her there he lays her face-up across the bed, head over the edge, stands astride her face, then bends over and picks her up, legs round his neck. She can return his kiss, but near orgasm she had far better slip him between her breasts or into her hand, and abandon herself to full orgasm.

The first genital kiss, to an inexperienced woman is another "situation". Kneeling before her, "*vers le buisson ardent des femmes*," looks fine, but one can't reach to do more than nuzzle. We suggest this: with the woman face-up along the bed, sit on the edge half-facing her feet. Kiss her all over, then reach over and pick up her farther leg and kiss her foot. Quickly slip your nearer elbow through her raised knee, open her, and kiss gently on the closed labia until she is ready for deeper and deeper tongue strokes. Fewer and fewer women are now inhibited about being kissed, though rather more can't get pleasure from kissing the man. A surprising number of women cannot initially be got there at all without prolonged genital kissing, a fact which Indian love books recognize. For a very shy woman (or man), try it in the dark – but certainly try it.

In the other direction, good mouthwork is perhaps one of the most valued gifts a woman can give and well worth practicing. A spontaneous genital kiss to a man is one of the most moving gestures in the whole sexual experience.

mouth music
One can give the woman dozens of orgasms in this way, and she may still want to go on from there.

variety

Plan your menus. Nobody wants a seven-course meal every time. At least seventy-five percent of really rewarding sex will be your absolutely straight, bedtime or morning pattern. For longer sessions, you need to be rested – weekends, holidays, and special occasions on impulse. If you make up your mind that over the course of time you'll try everything and have sex everywhere, the occasions will arise: when you feel one coming on, or know you will have the opportunity, plan together – with the book if you like – but don't expect necessarily to keep to what you outlined. Stick to it sometimes, however, so you don't miss things. Most couples will strike out perhaps a third of our suggestions as not turning them on, and pick up three or four headed "we must try that," if they haven't already.

Usually start with vaginal sex, move on to handwork, use mouthwork to get a further erection – maybe have a final orgasm by masturbating together. Prolonged spinouts involving

matrimonial

Uniquely satisfying in its adaptability to mood and the ideal quick-orgasm position.

make-believe, experiments, and so on often go best on waking
fresh – so do positions needing a very hard erection. Unlike a
man, an untired and responsive woman can afford to take
orgasms from any source in any order, unless her pattern is
one overwhelming orgasm only – if so, keep it for last. See
Come again.

Varying times of day is well worthwhile, but depends on
your commitments and how easily you can get some privacy or
clear your mind of other things, but try never to put it off if you
both want it, except to "save up" for something. Planning and
thinking about sex to come is part of love. So is lying together in
complete luxury afterwards.

matrimonial

Every culture has its own fads about best positions, and
experiment is essential. If we come back to the good old Adam
and Eve missionary position with him on top, astride or
between, and her underneath facing – and we do come back to
it – that is because it's uniquely satisfying. Chiefly it's unique in
its adaptability to mood; it can be wildly tough or very tender,
long or quick, deep or shallow.

Matrimonial is the starting point for nearly every sequence,
second only to the side positions, and the most reliable mutual
finishing-point for orgasm. If you start in it, you can deepen it
by raising her legs, move to the clitoris by putting one leg
between hers, roll about or right over, finishing with her on top,
kneel and lie back into the letter X with each partner lying
between the other's legs (see *X position*), move into back, side or
standing positions, then come back for the finish. It is also,
together with the deeper versions, the ideal quick-orgasm
position for both sexes. The only equally quick position for him
is from behind if she is very tight, and the only quicker for her is
astride on top. In fact, the chief reason for using the other 600
positions is to delay his final orgasm while multiplying hers.
Experimentation will show you which suit you best.

Even excluding the leg-raising variants, this position has
won more medals at international expositions than any other.
On the other hand, there is no one surefire sex position which
suits everyone. There are experienced women who never come
in this position, or only rarely: whether this is due to
unconscious forces or position of the vulva, which can be a
problem, doesn't matter a damn – try another position,
especially if the man is overweight. The matrimonial and all
deep or weightbearing positions are now known to be a bad
idea in pregnancy: a few non-pregnant non-responders have
had their lives changed by one or two hard pillows under the
buttocks. There are non-matrimoniable women who have to be
taken sitting, face to face, or from behind, finger to clitoris, or
who need to ride. If the man needs her flat to finish, give her
several orgasms in her preferred position first, then turn her. A

gentleman is defined as one who takes his weight on his hands. There are great advantages anyway in ending in a position where you can settle in each other's arms without exertion.

The tuning adjustments for matrimonials can be highly important – hard enough bed, use of pillows if she is slim or built that way. Bed, cushion, and flesh should between them give the consistency of buttocks which would be esthetically a bit too big. Tough or tender, how high you ride, pinned down (fold her arms gently up behind her and hold each of her thumbs in one of your hands) or not pinned down, astride her legs (holding them open by putting a foot under each of her insteps) or between them, spreading her with your legs – all make subtle differences. If your pubis isn't very hard and she needs a touch more clitoris, try a leg-between position or add finger contact. She can for her part hold your foreskin or penile shaft skin forcibly back with her hand (see *Florentine*).

missionary position

Name given by amused Polynesians, who preferred squatting intercourse, to the European matrimonial. Libel on one of the most rewarding sex positions.

upper hands

If the matrimonial is the king of postures, the queen is her turn on top, "riding St. George". Indian erotology is the only ancient tradition devoid of stupid patriarchal hangups about the need for her to be underneath, and unashamed about accepting her fully aggressive role in reciprocal sex. With a woman who has good vaginal muscle control it can be fantastic for the man, but for her it is unique, giving her total freedom to control movement, depth, and her partner. She can lean forward for breast or mouth kisses, back to show herself to him, touch her clitoris as she moves, delay if she wishes, for emphasis – the lot. She can also ride him facing or facing away, or turn from one into the other, once or often.

Riding postures need a stiff erection (or she may bend him painfully with an over-hurried insertion). This is in fact about the only kind of intercourse in which one or both can be injured by clumsiness or by slipping, so test yourselves gradually. Once in, she can go facing, backing, kneeling, sitting, crosslegged upon him. sideways, or round and round, and make movements in three dimensions and circularly with her hips. She can also lie on him (reversed matrimonial), legs astride or between. When she has taken her main orgasm, he can either turn her, or she can lie back astride him, head between his feet, without disconnecting, and go on in the letter X or the full matrimonial for his orgasm. Since it needs a stiff erection, and

upper hands
The queen of postures.

some women prefer to start from foreplay laterally or underneath, this makes a good second-figure of a series. If she wants to bring him to orgasm this way, they should try it first, preferably on waking and when he is fresh, with a hard waking erection.

The round-and-round and cinder-sifting motions of the woman's hips – what the French call the Lyons mail-coach (*la diligence de Lyon*) – come easily with practice if you've got the right personality.

frontal

All the face-to-face positions where one partner has both thighs between those of the other – he astride both hers or between them. Includes all the varieties of the matrimonial, plus most of the more complicated, deep facing positions. Gives more depth (usually), but less clitoral pressure than the *flanquettes*. To unscramble a complicated posture for purposes of classification, turn the partners round mentally and see if they can finish up face-to-face in a matrimonial without crossing legs. If so, it's frontal. If not, and they finish face-to-face astride one leg, it's a *flanquette*; square from behind (*croupade*); or from behind, astride a leg (*cuissade*). It's as simple as that.

This isn't an intellectual classificatory exercise. Postures are to be used in sequence, and one needs to make as few radical shifts, such as climbing over legs or turning a partner over, as possible – consider, in dancing, the difference between an impetus turn and a natural spin turn. This is important in planning sequences, though once you get used to going through five, 10 or 20 postures at a single session you'll do it automatically: at first, whichever partner leads, they need to envisage all the stages in getting where they are going to avoid clumsiness and breaks, other than natural and intended ones.

inversion

Not homosexuality, which isn't in our book, but taking him or her head-down. He can sit on a chair or stool, and take her astride facing – then she lies back until her head rests on a cushion on the floor. Or she can lie down, raising her hips – he stands between her legs and enters her either from in front or from behind while she rests on her elbows or walks on her hands (the wheelbarrow). He can lie over the edge of the bed, face up, while she sits or stands astride. With orgasm, the buildup of pressure in the veins of the face and neck can produce startling sensations. Unless you want a body on your hands, better not try this on a hypertensive executive – remember Attila the Hun's young concubine – but it should be safe enough if you're fit. It is the way to handle those idiotic

upper hands

*For her it is a unique
position, giving her total
freedom to control
movement and her partner.*

frontal
*Not one but a range
of positions for
deep penetration.*

people who try to persuade a lover to boost their orgasm by throttling them – if you meet one of these, never do anything so damned silly, but teach them this alternative and equally rewarding method. You may save two lives – hers, and, since most people's grip tightens in orgasm, her next boyfriend's, which could easily be spent in jail for homicide.

Inverted 69 is described elsewhere (see *Mouth music*). This makes a good tryout, always works if you can lift her, and will give her an idea of the quality of sensation involved; not everyone likes it.

inversion
For the young and fit – head down gives startling sensations at orgasm.

flanquette

The half-facing group of sexual postures – she lies facing him
with one of her legs between his, and consequently one of his
legs between hers, the frontal equivalent of the *Cuissades*. These
positions give extra clitoral pressure from the man's thigh if he
presses hard with it.

flanquette
*Half-facing, with the
possibility of extra
clitoral pressure.*

x position

A winner for prolonged slow intercourse. Start with her sitting facing astride him, penis fully inserted. She then lies right back until each partner's head and trunk are between the other's wide-open legs, and they clasp hands. Slow, coordinated wriggling movements will keep him erect and her close to orgasm for long periods. To switch back to other positions, either of them can sit up without disconnecting.

x position
For slow, drawn-out intercourse, this is a winner.

standing postions

The traditional upright is a quickie, and apt to produce stiff male muscles unless she is tall. Many women need to stand on two thick phone directories with the yellow pages, or an equivalent. Best undertaken up against a solid object such as a wall or a tree (not a door, whichever way it opens). Alternatively, you can be free standing, legs apart for stability and arms clasped round each other's buttocks – looking down as you move can be really sensual.

There are two kinds of position – this one, subject to a good match in height, and the Hindu versions where he picks her up: these are tremendous if she is light as an Oriya dancing girl, otherwise they need to be executed in water to make her weightless (see *Bathing*). For a tall woman, try with her arms round your neck, one of her feet on the ground, and the other over your elbow. She can then go legs around waist, both legs over your arms, and even both legs round your neck, lying back, if you are strong enough, into a head-down position. Try this over a bed in case you drop her, but stand on a firm floor, not a mattress. If you are back up to a wall, she can swing herself with one foot. Not good orgasm positions – designed

standing
(left and right) If your relative heights and her weight permit, these variants extend coition for both partners.

rather to spin out coition. Standing positions from behind need no special comment – she needs to lean over or hold onto something rigid.

If you have real height problems, try the upright positions on a flight of stairs. The head-down genital kiss is a winner if you are strong enough to hold her up, and she takes a good leg grip.

rear entry

The other human option – for most mammals, it's the only one. Works admirably standing, lying, kneeling, sitting, or with the woman astride. The lack of face-to-faceness is more than compensated for by extra depth and buttock stimulation, hand access to breasts and clitoris, and the sight of a pretty rear view. For the standing positions, she needs something of the right height to support her; in the head-down kneeling positions, you need to be careful not to push her face into the mattress; and in all of the deep variants you need to avoid going too deep too hard, or you will hit an ovary, which is as painful as hitting a testicle. A few women are put off by the symbolism – "doing it like animals," "not being valued if we aren't face to face" – but the physical payoff is so intense that they shouldn't allow these feelings to make them miss it. They could try it first with the man lying on his back and the woman lying faceup on top of him, or kneeling astride facing away, though these don't give the unique depth and total perineal stimulation of the rear kneeling positions (see *Négresse*). The man can hold her breasts or pubis, or, if she likes to be controlled, grasp her wrists behind her. A pile of hard pillows under her middle will help to prevent the position collapsing if she doesn't like being forcibly held, or she can kneel on the floor with her chest on the bed or a chair-seat. The head-down position is best for depth and total apposition – avoid it if it hurts her, or if she has a weak back, or if she is pregnant. Some women like a finger on the clitoris during intercourse, either his or hers, and this is easy in all rear positions. It's worth trying in any case, as it totally alters the range of sensation. Grasping the whole pussy in one hand gives a different sensation again and doesn't give the excessive sharpness which comes from strong clitoral stimulation. Or you can withdraw briefly and give a few clitoral strokes with the glans, guiding it with your hand.

While the deep kneeling position is, or can be, one of the toughest, from behind on your sides is about the gentlest (*à la paresseuse* – the lazy position) and can even be done in sleep – best if she draws her top thigh up a little and sticks her bottom out. This is one position which, in many women, can be managed with very little or even no erection; it can help to cure partial impotence or nervousness on the male side by restoring morale. It's also excellent if you want it gentle for health reasons. It's well worth experimenting with the full range of

rear entry
*works admirably standing,
lying, kneeling or sitting.*

rear positions at least as fully as with the face-to-face series, because there will be at least one you'll almost certainly use regularly along with the matrimonial, and its variants, and the woman-astride positions.

rear entry

Start gently, for with excess vigor in this deep position you might hit an ovary.

postillionage

Putting a finger in or on your partner's anus just before orgasm. Popular in French erotic books, and works on some people. Most prefer firm finger pressure just in front of the anus; in men, this can produce an erection used alone. Use a small vibrator rather than a finger if you prefer – and don't put either into the vagina afterwards, if you've actually inserted it. Firm pressure with a heel behind the scrotum or between anus and vulva works as well in some postures.

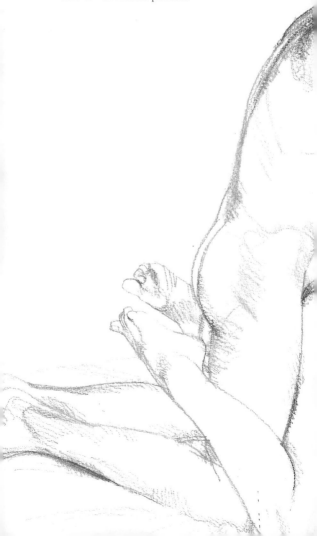

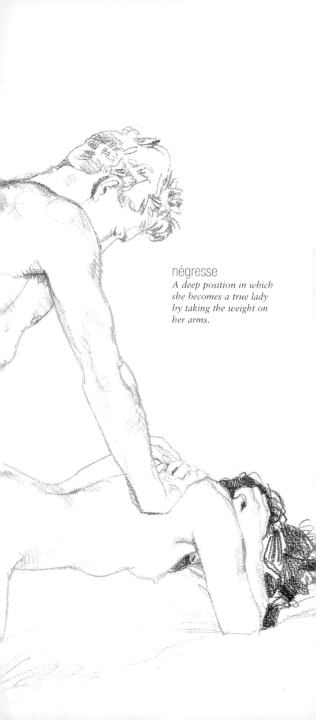

négresse
A deep position in which she becomes a true lady by taking the weight on her arms.

croupade
Squarely from behind.

négresse

Taking the woman from behind. She kneels, hands clasped
behind her neck, breasts and face on the bed. He kneels behind.
She hooks her legs over his and pulls him to her with them – he
puts a hand on each of her shoulder blades and presses down.
Very deep position – apt to pump her full of air which escapes
later in a disconcerting manner – otherwise excellent.

croupade

Any position in which he takes her squarely from behind, i.e. all
rear-entry positions except those where she has one leg between
his or is half-turned on her side (see *Cuissade*).

cuissade

The half-rear entry positions, where she turns her back to him
and he enters with one of her legs between his and the other
more or less drawn up: in some versions, she lies half-turned on
her side for him, still facing away.

cuissade
Half-rear, half-side entry.

florentine

Coitus *à la florentine*: intercourse with the woman holding the man's penile skin (and foreskin if he has one) forcibly back with finger and thumb at the root of the penis and keeping it stretched all the time, both in and out. Excellent way of speeding up ejaculation, and greatly boosts intensity of male sensation if you get the tension right.

saxonus

Coitus *saxonus* – pressing firmly on the male urethra near the root of the penis to prevent ejaculation and (hopefully) conception. No use as a contraceptive, since sperm is around

long before he ejaculates – but some women do have the knack, during masturbation, of stopping and restarting ejaculation by urethral pressure so as to spin out the male peak.

This is best done by pressing on the shaft near the root with two or three fingers, but you need to press hard (don't bruise). Some people press midway between scrotum and anus. The idea is to allow ejaculation to occur piecemeal. If you stop it altogether, he will eventually ejaculate into the bladder. There's no evidence that this is harmful unless done violently and often, but it's probably better avoided. Interrupting ejaculation is also probably harmless, but it is difficult and won't work on everyone. Women who have this as a party piece say it is appreciated, but that may depend on their partner. You might as well stop just short of ejaculation, then restart the whole business a few minutes later.

florentine
Intense sensations for him, and a quick finish.

pompoir

The most sought-after feminine sexual response of all.

"She must . . . close and constrict the Yoni until it holds the Lingam as with a finger, opening and shutting at her pleasure, and finally acting as the hand of the Gopala-girl who milks the cow. This can be learned only by long practice, and especially by throwing the will into the part affected, even as men endeavor to sharpen their hearing . . . Her husband will then value her above all women, nor would he exchange her for the most beautiful queen in the Three Worlds. . . . Among some races the *constrictor vaginae* muscles are abnormally developed. In Abyssinia, for instance, a woman can so exert them as to cause pain to a man, and, when sitting on his thighs, she can induce orgasm without moving any other part of her person. Such an artist is called by the Arabs Kabbazah, literally, a holder, and it is not surprising that slave dealers pay large sums for her."

Thus Richard Burton. It has nothing to do with "race", but a lot to do with practice. See *Exercises*.

birdsong at morning

What your partner says in orgasm should never be quoted at him or her – it can be played back when you are both in a suitable mood, but only then. It's the time when people are spiritually most naked.

There is a striking consistency, over ages and continents, in what women say in orgasm. Japanese, Indian, French, and English all babble about dying ("Some of them," said Abbé Brantôme, "yell out 'I'm dying,' but I think they enjoy that sort of death"), about Mother (they often call for her at the critical moment), and about religion, even if they are atheists. This is natural – orgasm is the most religious moment of our lives, of which all other mystical kicks are a mere translation. Men are apt to growl like bears, or utter aggressive monosyllables like "In, In, In!" The wife of the Leopard in the novel of the same name used to yell out "Gesumaria!" and there is an infinite variety of sounds short of speech.

Why these cries are so charming in both sexes it's hard to say. The Indians classified them, compared them to bird-cries, and warned how easily parrots and mynahs pick them up, with bad social vibrations when they repeat the lesson – hence no parrots in the love chamber. It is important to learn to read them while enjoying the music, and in particular to know when "Stop" means stop and when it means "For God's sake, go on." This is an individual language, and you need to be a sensitive field observer to learn its meaning.

Some of the "words" are common – a gasp when a touch registers right, a shuddering out-breath when you follow

pompoir
*If a woman has this knack,
"Her husband will value her
above all women ..."*

birdsong at morning

*It is best to keeps mynahs
out of the bedroom – they
pick up the strange cries of
people at orgasm.*

through. Women, and some men, talk continuously in a sort of baby-whisper, or repeat four-letter words of the most unlikely kind – some you can hear several blocks away, while others still are dead silent or laugh or sob disconcertingly. Of the really noisy performers, some like to be allowed to yell, while others like to be gagged, or stuff their hair in their mouths in the style of a Japanese print (traditional Japanese houses have paper partitions). Men can be equally noisy in the run-up to orgasm, but are not usually so continuously vocal.

The important point is this: in mutual, let-go intercourse, make as much noise as you like. It is curious that we need to write this down, but house and hotel designers haven't yet realized it – they all seem to be married to noiseless, childless partners, or they'd avoid plasterboard. Totally silent intercourse, with each partner's hand firmly over the other's mouth, can be fun if you simply can't risk being overheard. Another variation is to have two kinds of intercourse at once – straight, gentle coitus, while each partner describes some other much wilder proceeding in fantasy, perhaps for next time. The fantasy can be as wild as you like. This is the place to experience things you can't possibly act out, and to learn your partner's fantasy needs. These fantasies can be heterosexual, homosexual, incestuous, tender, wild, or bloodthirsty – don't block, and don't be afraid of your partner's fantasy; this is a dream you are in. But be careful about recording such dreams, as they can be disturbing at the daylight level. Let them go with the release of orgasm.

Lovers who really know one another won't be frightened or take advantage. If you do find this double nakedness disturbing, set rules – practicable or happy fantasies only. Never, never refer to pillow talk in anger later on ("I always knew you were a lesbian, etc."). This is contemptible. Fantasy apart, the only really disturbing manifestation of love-music is when the woman laughs uncontrollably – some do. Don't be uptight about this. She isn't laughing at you.

little death

La petite mort: some women do indeed pass right out, the "little death" of French poetry. Men occasionally do the same. The experience is not unpleasant, but it can scare an inexperienced partner cold. A friend of ours had this happen with the first girl he ever slept with. On recovery, she explained, "I'm awfully sorry, but I always do that." By then he had called the police and the ambulance. So there is no cause for alarm, any more than over the yells, convulsions, hysterical laughter, or sobbing, or any of the other quite unexpected reactions which go with complete orgasm in some people. By contrast, others simply shut their eyes, but enjoy it no less. Sound and fury can be a flattering testimonial to a partner's skills, but a fallacious one, because they don't depend on the intensity of feeling, nor it upon them.

Men don't very often pass right out – that's her privilege – though they can give a splendid impersonation of a fit. In any case, you'll soon get to know your partner's pattern once you're past any initial shocks.

come again

Not all can, but we are sure that far more could than actually do, men especially.

Multiple orgasm comes easily to many if not all women if they are responsive enough and care to go on, either with intercourse or afterplay, after one orgasm; that is, really responsive women who definitely fall in the once-and-it's-over category like men are fairly rare. Some women get one continuous series of orgasms with no single, big peak. Responsiveness is beyond analysis, a subtle mixture of physiology, mood, culture, upbringing, and having the man she wants. Therefore, if you can get one really intense climax, you could probably get more if you went on. The chief exceptions are those who are fragile and tire easily, or who want to savor the period of intense relaxation after each orgasm rather than switch to a new kind of stimulation.

With men it is more complicated still. Some can get six or more full orgasms in a few hours provided they aren't timestressed and don't attempt it daily. Some can do it daily. Others can't get a second erection for a set time. It pays to establish this time early on – it may be shorter than you think. Whether it is alterable nobody knows – nor yet whether individual differences depend on physical or mental factors, though certainly a great many men have been hocussed by talk about sex being exhausting into a performance below what they could manage.

Since exercise and practice improve almost all performances, it would be odd if they didn't improve this one. In any case, it's not, for the man, the number of orgasms that matter – most men can get a second by slow handwork and a third from self-stimulation within an hour of full intercourse – it is rather the ability either to hold off your own orgasm as long as you want, or to go on after, or soon after it, even if you don't come a second time. Failing this one can't take a woman the whole way in unsupplemented intercourse. Many lovers don't try, but switch their techniques to economize – yet even so it's not the same unless you manage to finish, if not together, at least fairly close together.

Ability to hold and to repeat is particularly important to the many (usually over-continent) males who have hair-trigger trouble. Don't let it become a self-aggravating worry. It matters not a jot provided you can get another erection inside half an hour – there are plenty of other things to do while you are waiting. Avoid performance anxiety: instead, find out by trial just how soon you can get a serviceable erection again – usually this will be long-lasting and won't end in a full climax, but will enable you to give her 10, 20, or more minutes of full intercourse while you concentrate on her.

If he can't, doesn't, or is worried about it, it is no use reasoning with him. You, Madam, must take over. Full technical details are given under *Hairtrigger trouble*. If you look disappointed, you'll have had it for the night and possibly for keeps. Suggest some diversionary entertainment, give him half an hour, then stiffen him yourself by hand- and mouthwork. Tell him out of hours what you intend doing; you want to see how soon he can get stiff again (otherwise it looks as though you were unsatisfied, and he'll feel guilty and switch himself off). Bring this off neatly and you'll have added a new dimension to both your lives. Two important points: one, immediately after a full orgasm, some men can't stand any genital stimulation – they feel it as intense pain. If he is like this, give him a half hour or more. Two, if he really is uptight about it, quite a few women can be perfectly well penetrated with the merest half-erection if taken from behind on their side. Once started like this, full erection usually follows.

Some men when tired can't get an erection but can ejaculate

come again
Waking the dead.

on hand- or mouthwork: others get an erection which lasts indefinitely, but can't reach orgasm. This last sort, who are actually slow, not fast, responders, make sexual athletes. Whether it can be cultivated as a choice isn't clear, but abundant sex and a certain amount of masturbatory training in holding back a climax will help. Most over-fast responders are having sex far too rarely. See *Frequency*.

Corpse revivers: the best are skillful manual and oral work and direct suction. A woman can carefully take not only the penis but the whole scrotum as well into her mouth and hold them with her lips, then suck firmly on the penis itself while pressing with a finger at its root behind. Then, when she feels stiffening, she can switch to in and out movements. Vigorous masturbation will always produce a second ejaculation in time, even if it doesn't produce a serviceable erection. Some couples, all passion spent but still wanting one more orgasm before finishing, like to lie facing and watch one another as they bring themselves to climax. This is an added experience, not a confession of defeat, and can be immensely and unexpectedly exciting. See *Handwork*.

relaxation

It is probably the general experience, and we have been assuming here, that maximum feeling in orgasm goes with maximum muscular tension. A great many techniques (postures, bondage, and so on) are designed to boost this tension. On the other hand, it is by no means universally true. The orgasm of total relaxation is rather harder to manage, largely because it cannot be boosted artificially, but is both different and, when it works, overwhelming. There are also some people, chiefly women, for whom tension seems actively to interfere with full response.

We've seen ideological writings about this which infer, for example, that tension orgasms represent fear of full release, latent sadism, and so on. One writer opined that yells, grimaces, and convulsions indicate fear and pain, rather than love and pleasure – presumably he had never seen himself making love, or had never had a wild orgasm. In fact, the only universal generalization about sex seems to be that no one pattern fits everyone. How far these differences between people depend on physiology and how far on latent aggression and the like is probably not a practically important question – some need one, and some the other. Our point is that with practice most people can widen their repertoire by learning to use both, and sense the needs of the moment so as to alternate them, thereby doubling their range of physical sensation and making sex still more communicative. Certainly some tension represents fear of letting go, and some people prefer to be "forced," voluntarily, to accept orgasms – in this case, initially at least, it's probably sensible to make use of the responses you have. If you recognize this kind of reaction, however, don't omit to try the other mode. Mammals seem to vary, according to species, between fight-and-rape-type mating and a version in which the female appears near-indifferent, so there isn't much to be learned from zoology in this context.

The straight, sleepy, non-special intercourse, on your side or in the matrimonial position, is relaxed, but this isn't what we mean. In going for a fully relaxed orgasm, either one partner is totally passive and the other a soloist, or both achieve a state of non effort in which wholly automatic movements – internal, for the woman – take over. Try both kinds – it is easier initially to work up both modes together.

Probably the easiest initial method is for the less active partner in ordinary intercourse (this usually but not always means the one underneath) to try stopping all movement just as the orgasmic buildup begins and go completely limp (warn your partner first). Some people do this naturally: if you have had any relaxation training, starting by letting one finger get heavy and so on, use the same technique here.

You may find that on the first few occasions the fact of trying produces a different sort of tension, but after a few attempts most easily-stimulated people can learn to let their orgasm happen, and will find that this feels different from the equally pleasant orgasm one produces either by trying, or by struggling and postponing. Don't postpone – don't, in fact, be active at all. Then practice the same kind of relaxation while your partner masturbates or sucks you. The movements he or she makes will be physically the same as for "slow masturbation" as we've described it, but the operator is looking for quite different feedback – in the "hard" version, whether the partner is tied or free, you are deliberately holding back or forcing them on, keeping just that much out of step with their reactions. In the "soft" version you need to be a fraction ahead of those reactions so that they don't need to move or struggle. The difference can't be described, only felt. Practically, it means a quicker, steadier rhythm of stimulation – no slow teasing and no sudden bursts – you are making it and they are letting it happen.

Once you have got this right in intercourse and in other kinds of stimulation, including all the extras we've mentioned, you can go on to "motionless" coitus. It won't, of course, initially be entirely motionless, but try, after the first round of gentle movement, what happens if you stop thinking.

relaxation
The sense of fusion that can result from near motionless intercourse is unparalleled.

Movements of a sort will continue, but in time and with practice get less and less voluntary, especially if the woman has good vaginal muscle control. Ultimately, some people learn to insert and do nothing, but still reach an orgasm in which they totally fuse, giving a sensation of being a single person – not describable, again, and probably not always realizable, but fantastic when it happens.

We should stress that this doesn't involve going slow, holding back, or any other voluntary intervention. If you find it not working, switch back to ordinary movements, but without taking too much thought – sometimes you will both sense that the moment has come to shift position and go all out for a big one; complete fusion isn't biddable, and ordinary, athletic sex is fine. If it does happen, the sensation is so extraordinary you will want to repeat it.

Reliable relaxation, and the almost frightening self-loss that goes with it, are what most sexual yogis have aimed at, except that they usually tried not to ejaculate. Some of these sexual mystics recommend a special relaxed posture (man on his left side, woman on her back at right-angles, knees drawn up, legs bridging his hips, feet flat on the bed). Whether this helps may well depend on your build. What is worth suggesting, even for people who can't totally relax, is that they play through all the techniques we have described, aiming at relaxation instead of maximum tension and adjusting their feedback accordingly. Similarly people who naturally relax in intercourse should try occasionally to play it for full tension – just as women who like to thrash around should sometimes try being forcibly held still, and vice versa.

This sort of experimentation against one's built-in response is better value in widening one's range of lovemaking than mechanical variations of posture or trying out gadgets and stunts. It is one part of lovemaking which requires effort beyond mere curiosity, but it's essential if you hope to go as far in making sex communicate as you are physically and mentally able.

waking

She says: "Sleep patterns matter, and it's the man who wakes with an erection. While it's great to be woken in the middle of the night with intercourse, this doesn't apply when one has had a ghastly day and has an interview coming up next morning; use some sense. It also doesn't apply in the middle of a dream one has to finish." Some women take minutes or hours to wake up, and though they enjoy gentle intercourse waking – and it works far better than an alarm clock – don't expect athletics. The trouble is that this is the time when many males are ready for them and expect to be ridden, masturbated, sucked, and what have you. Keep these early waking workouts for Sundays and holidays, and preferably make coffee first, erection or no erection. Some people are lucky in having roughly the same sleeping hours, but if one were early and the other a night person that, too, could well give rise to real problems. If you have these, talk about them; some people do use sleep as an excuse for avoiding intercourse, but between lovers who are on different clocks it can be real and doesn't imply rejection.

If you have children, you have to be ready to be woken by them, and restrict yourselves accordingly. Don't lock them out. Rearrange your sex life to get the necessary privacy at other times – if all else fails, get a baby-sitter and stay at a motel once a month. The sound and fury of really ongoing sex would give primal scene problems to any small child, so don't take risks; the sort of sex we have, and are talking about here, almost excludes fertility – it's a choice one may have to make, while houses and family structure are as they are.

waking
Waking next to someone and being pleased they're there is as much part of lovemaking as an early morning workout.

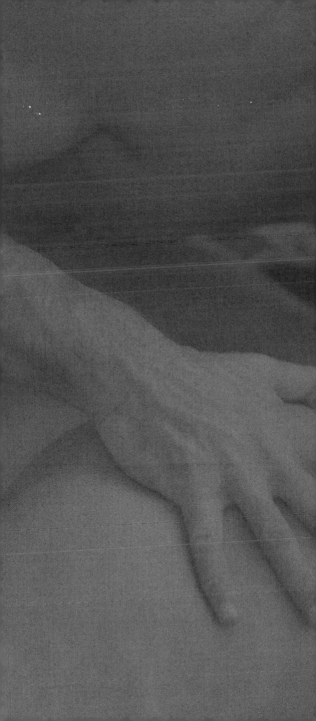

sauces

playtime

We have said this before, but we repeat: sex is the most important sort of adult play. If you can't relax here, you never will. Don't be scared of psychodrama. Be the Sultan and his favorite concubine, the burglar and the maiden, even a dog and a currant bun, anything you fancy for the hell of it. Take off your shell along with your clothes.

A few people are immensely excited by having sex with the assistance of the oldest human dramatic expedient – a mask, which suppresses you and makes you someone else (see *Masks*). Most of us can learn to do the same change without it, and when this comes the complete mental nakedness between you is the most exhilarating sort of nudism – so complete that one is healthily scared of it at first. Getting unscared is probably the most important lesson of sex. Don't use alcohol for this – it's a neutering drug. Real sex release, when one achieves it, is what marijuana, alcohol, etc, are substitutes for.

So let him be a Roman, or a gangster, or a woman, or a dog, and let her be a virgin, or a slave, or a Sultana, or Lolita, or indeed anything which turns either of you on. You weren't self-

conscious about this when you were three – grow backward again in an adult context. The rules are only those of childplay – if it gets nasty, or spiteful, or unhappy, stop the game: while it stays wild and exciting, it has a climax children's games lack; that is the privilege of play when you are adult.

chinese style

This is described in the classical treatises, and is remarkably like uninhibited European sex. The best thing about this style is the delightful names given to postures: "Wailing Monkey Clasping a Tree," "Wild Geese Flying on their Backs," for two quite ordinary positions (seated face to face; woman on top facing away). The main elaboration consists in various complicated mixtures of deep and shallow strokes, often in magical numbers – five deep, eight shallow, and so on. Intercourse is performed naked, on a Chinese bed, in the open air, or on the floor and the woman treated far less as an equal in sex than in Indian erotology. Mystical schools tried to avoid ejaculation (see *Karezza*).

playtime
Getting unscared, through play, is probably the most important lesson of sex.

indian style

Now widely familiar from the *Kama Sutra*, the *Koka Shastra* and
so on. Intercourse on a bed or on cushions, fully naked, but with
the woman wearing all her ornaments. Many complicated
positions, including some derived from yoga which aim to
avoid ejaculation (see *Karezza*), standing positions, and woman-
on-top positions (*purushayita*) which are regarded as specially
devout, since in Tantric Hinduism she is Energy and he is
Immanence. All, if you do it in the original spirit and not for
variety only, intimately linked with the Indian love of living at
several levels – not only sex, but also meditative technique in
which one attempts to be subjectively both male and female for
mystical purposes, or modified dance in which, beside making
love, one acts out a scene from the hagiography of Vishnu and
his *Avatars*, or the *Life of Rama*. There is a section on sexual
technique in the chief classical dance treatise – dancers were
temple maidens or *devadasis* who gave themselves to the devout
as part of a religious exercise. Difficult for us to recapture, in
spite of a dawning awareness of the psychoanalytic rightness of
much Hindu intuition.

Specialities include love-cries (see *Birdsong at morning*), love-
blows (struck with fingertips on one another's breast, back,
buttocks, and genitals), lovebites as tokens of possession, and
erotic scratchmarks – much skin stimulation with specially
grown, long fingernails, from mere brushing to a passionate
scratch (classically confined to the armpit and the "girdle path"
– pantie region – where marks won't show in Indian day dress).

Of all the Indian techniques, the standing postures are
probably the best worth learning, if the woman is light enough.
Few women who weren't trained from birth could, for example,
stand leaning backwards on feet and hands, limbo-style, then
put their arms round their legs and their head between their
thighs, so as to take alternate strokes in mouth and vagina –
or manage the one-leg-standing, one-leg-around-waist poses
cultivated by temple girls. The best Indian accomplishment, the
full pompoir, comes from the Tamil South, and unfortunately
isn't taught in the texts, though the *devadasis* learned it from
their mothers. See *Pompoir*, *Exercises*.

japanese style

Intercourse on the floor or on cushions, as with most oriental
styles: partial nakedness only, numerous squatting and semi-
squatting positions, a lot of bondage, a lot of preoccupation
with extras and odd devices. We're talking here about the sexual
customs known from eighteenth- and early nineteenth-century
prints. What would be hard to copy is the essentially Japanese
mixture of violence and formality, which does not sit easily with
our tradition of tenderness. Other differences are: elaborate
finger-stimulation of the woman, thumb in anus, fingers in

vagina; and a big range of mechanical devices – a glans cap of hard material (*kabutogata*), penile-shaft tubes (*do-gata*), some of them latticed (*yoroi-gata*), or with a glans cap as well (*yaso-gata*); dildoes (*engi*), often strapped to the woman's heel, while her ankle is held up to a sling round her neck to give a better swing to the movement; thongs to bind tightly round the penile shaft, rendering it both rough and permanently stiff enough for insertion (*higozuiki*); and merkins to hold in the hand (*azuma-gata*). Postures cover the whole range, but the lovers of the "floating world" greatly enjoy the simulation of rape – what George Moore called "furious fornications" – where the artistic emphasis is on huge parts, copious secretions, and so on: sex is played hard in this tradition.

turkish style

The Sultan of the Ottoman empire, so far from living "*mit Saus und Braus,*" was the bottom man of a huge pyramid of functionaries and eunuchs, who lived in fear of his life and was obliged to sign a stud-book at each act of sex. Often he had

chinese style
If nothing else, this will give you new names for old positions.

spent his youth in the company of mistresses known to be sterile, while waiting to know if he would reign or be strangled at the accession of another heir. His innumerable harem were taught the arts of pleasing, but these are not recorded. The chosen lady would enter his bedchamber naked, and in darkness dive under the covers at the bed foot, wriggling her way up alongside him to wait his pleasure. Recalcitrant newcomers were brought in by the Aga Bashi with their thumbs tightly tied behind, and frequently beaten into submission by flogging the soles of their feet. Delinquent concubines were drowned in sacks – silk ones if they were *kadins*.

In spite of the facts, Turkish erotic scenes were a great nineteenth-century fantasy in Christian Europe. They need not be so biased towards the male – she can equally well be Gulbeyaz receiving a chosen Christian stud. Take it in turns.

south slav style

Well documented because of the very rich erotic folksong repertoire of the Balkans. Intercourse naked, with emphasis on the importance of genital perfume as a stimulus.

There are several reputedly "national" positions or approaches. Serbian intercourse (*Srpski jeb*) is mock rape – you throw her down, seize one ankle in each hand, and raise them over her head, then enter her with your full weight (do this on something soft – the traditional bare earth is beyond a game). Croatian intercourse (*hrvatski jeb*) is a woman's ploy – an elaborate tongue bath, with the man free or staked out, followed after leisurely stimulation by riding him astride (reputed by local wiseacres to be "exhausting"). The Lion position is a male masturbation method – squat down, heels to scrotum, place the penis between your ankles, rest on buttocks and hands, and move legs together. The style is passionate and affectionate, as befits a race of bride-stealing warriors whose women were natural partisans: tough plus tender.

substitutes

Handwork and oral love aren't substitutes for vaginal intercourse, but techniques on their own. The listed "substitutes" are what Europeans formerly used as contraceptive techniques which would ejaculate the male without masturbation and were less taboo than oral sex. The old "substitutes" have their place – some, like mammary intercourse, can be fully bilateral and all are occasionally fun – during a period, for example, or if she is very pregnant.

The *Paradis Charnels* of 1903 gives nine sites: hands (she joins her hands, thumbs crossed, fingers interlaced, and makes him a vagina, wetting her palms first with saliva   an old way of ending straight intercourse without risking pregnancy, though it isn't in fact a safe contraceptive method), mouth, between the thighs (see *Femoral intercourse*), the breasts, the armpit, and also the fold of the elbow and the knee. The other two substitute sites are the hair (long hair or plaits can be rolled into a vagina, or the penis lassooed with a loop of it, though some women may object because it's a bore to wash. Such techniques might be helpful for "safe sex".

karezza

The Alice Stockham treatment – going on and on and on while avoiding male orgasm.

This is really an exercise directed against hairtrigger trouble, rather than a general coital technique. Long intercourse is great, but the aim will be to ejaculate eventually. Enormously satisfying for the woman: the original Stockham version, where the male didn't ejaculate, but allowed his erection to subside inside the vagina has no conceivable advantage over going on equally long with orgasm, and is likely to spoil eventual response. Worth knowing about, however, if you read accounts of sex yoga drawn from Eastern sources. The old Tantric–Taoist system held that semen was spiritual gasoline – the man should be careful to conserve it while drawing "virtue" from the woman. One ejaculation could dissipate this supposed virtue. Accordingly, a great many sexual yogic positions in which movement was difficult were designed specifically for this kind of maneuver – giving the woman several orgasms while the man conserved his semen and performed what was in fact a meditative sexual exercise. Adept yogis also trained themselves to ejaculate internally – an unrewarding technique which deposits the semen in the bladder, whence it is passed with the urine: occasionally the same trick appears spontaneously as a disability and is difficult to unlearn. This explains the low male satisfaction value of many of the most elaborate Hindu positions. If you intend to use intercourse as a meditative technique, you may well use them, but there seems no rational ground against eventual ejaculation in any case.

Karezza was developed, possibly with similar ideas, by the Oneida community: it also kept conceptions down, albeit not over-reliably, as semen can leak without ejaculation. There was formerly an offbeat French priest who canvassed the same idea, as an answer to Vatican scruples over birth control, under the title of *continence conjugale*, but the idea failed to catch on. The method consists in total control of male movement – allowing the woman internal movements only and the man sufficient strokes to maintain erection, stopping as soon as tension mounts. Use it solely as a training technique for long intercourse, then switch to full movement and mutual orgasm, for which the woman will be fully ready. See *Pompoir*.

south slav style
*It's vigorous and no-nonsense,
but does not lack warmth.*

horse

The horse is an erotic object (see *Clothes*), and playing at horses, as well as riding them, notoriously turns some people on. One aficionado was Aristotle, who is frequently shown being ridden horseback-style by a girl friend. Medieval moralists who took this as an awful warning miss the point.

Men also like to dress women up as horses, though they can't usually be ridden in this manner. This seems at least as good a turn-on as disguising them as rabbits. Mentioned here for completeness – it's not our kick – but the game (*equus eroticus*, pony-girl game) figures in the literature. Either sex can be the steed. Odd how often children's games and grown-up sex games converge. Some people purchase a whole outfit including bit, saddle, etc. See firsthand description in *The Nightclerk*.

goldfish

Two naked people tied and put on a mattress together to make love fish-fashion, i.e. no hands. Originally a nineteenth-century bordel joke. It can be done (if you are the victims, try on your sides from behind). Venerable party game, but don't play it with strangers or leave the players unsupervised, even briefly. There was a nice spoof of this sex stunt in the movie *Soldier Blue*. A good many women can get an orgasm solo in this way simply by struggling, especially if you put them in front of a mirror. Don't both tie yourselves, even if you can manage it – you might not be able to get loose.

viennese oyster

A woman who can cross her feet behind her head, lying on her back, of course. When she has done so, you hold her tightly round each instep with your full hand and squeeze, lying on her full-length. Don't try to put an unsupple partner into this position – it can't be achieved by brute force. You can get a very similar sensation – unique rocking pelvic movement – with less expertise if she crosses her ankles on her tummy, knees to shoulders, and you lie on her crossed ankles with your full weight. Why "Viennese" we don't know. Tolerable for short periods only, but gives tremendous genital pressure for both.

clothes

It is part of the recovery from puritanism that most people now make love naked and most lovers sleep naked. Clothes, when they are worn, are there to be taken off – making love can very

well start by undressing one another, or by one partner
stripping for the other. Womens' magazines and tapes now give
what amount to courses on burlesque-type stripping as a
conventional turn-on for the man, but this use of clothing is a
conventional routine – for a start, it need not be the woman who
strips. Each partner, moreover, should practice removing the
clothes of the other sex without clumsiness or hold-ups, and
preferably with one hand.

Clothes and their removal as a kick have, if one wants to be
serious about it, a whole biology in terms of "releasers", a
releaser being what turns somebody on. The releasers for the
male are garments which emphasize breasts and buttocks, or,
like tight panties, "simplify the outline" of the female. Women
are not so dependent on this sort of concrete signalling – having
the right man is their chief releaser, a social and emotional one –
but many of them have preferences. A well-filled jockstrap or a
man naked from the waist down can act as part of the
preliminary scenery, and habitual nudity in bed and about the
house doesn't blunt these natural reactions.

Quite apart from this, some people react very strongly to
particular clothing situations on a lock-and-key basis – usually
these are men, occasionally women. This is the basis of kinky
fashions. Exactly what works on a particular person is highly
individual; in this case, he often knows and will ask for it. These
clothing turn-ons work exactly as a salmon-fly works for the
salmon. A bunch of feathers doesn't look like anything the
salmon eats (and when one fishes for them at salmon run they
aren't feeding in any case), but it combines a whole range of
unrelated stimuli which excite curiosity, aggression, and enough
other fishy emotions to provoke a strike. Human turn-ons are
equally complicated. How they become programmed in a given
individual isn't known, but there is an identifiable repertoire of
components, like the repertoire of feathers one can use in a lure
from which most of these stimuli are made. Superskin is one –
tightness, shininess, and texture; super-genitalness – firm pubis,
space between the thighs, extra pubic hair; mild threat –
blackness, leatheriness, sadistic-looking buckles; submission –
tied-upness, slave-bangles; and the suggestion of genitals
elsewhere – red lips, emphasis on the feet, which have "some
symmetry with that which thou dost crave"; shininess and
tinkling-earrings; chains; womanness – tiny waist, big breasts
and buttocks, long hair. And so on. Humans love to fool around
with the body image and alter it.

Others are textures – wetness, fur, rubber, plastic, leather.
Many people respond slightly to all of these, and this is another
basis of sexual fashion. Some respond so strongly to a few that
they don't hit full sexual function without them, but the
selection is highly individual, far more so than taste in food,
and to tie your fly you have to know your salmon. Every such
lure has at least three layers – tight, shiny, black leather is a
superskin with a womany smell; it also suggests acceptance of
the aggression of sex. Tiny, tight g-strings stress but hide her
pussy, hold her perfume so she can be kissed through them, and

suggest wicked, sexy girls rather than chaste sister-figures. Corsets make her hourglass-shaped and suggest tightness and helplessness. And so on. A horse, seen from behind, is a male "releaser" – it has long hair, big buttocks, and a teetering walk. A cow isn't.

Prostitutes, who know all this elementary biology, use all these lures, or dress one of them and catch fish who respond to it. Many woman have similar turn-ons themselves, but some tend to be a bit scared of them as kinky, and, in particular, to feel "he's in love with gloves or black lingerie, not with me." This is the wrong approach. If your man has a physical turn-on, it has nothing to do with his valuation of you, and he will love you more the more skillfully you sense and use it. Turn-ons are not choosable – he has them or he hasn't. If he has them, you can catch your favorite fish at every cast. Don't try to turn yourself into something you're not. You need to feel comfortable when responding to your partner's turn-ons. But, if he has a preference you can meet, you are unstoppable. The "you" part is in letting him see you sense it and meet it. If you, too, have turn-ons, tell him, and use them.

Accordingly, the same tactic applies here as for sexual fantasies generally. Uninhibited partners will tell each other about them (try free-associating just before orgasm if you are shy). Really communicating partners look for them and put them on the menu unannounced – there is no more complete communication. As with other fantasies, if the thing itself doesn't turn you on equally, the response will. Infantile, symbolic, fetishistic, and generally wild fantasies are part of love, and only a problem if they take up too much time and start spoiling the full reciprocity of sex (see Fetishes). For most people they don't, and a great many people of both sexes have them. No matter how odd, they are usually rewarding – more so than ties or candy as anniversary presents. People are still rightly shy about their innermost mind-life; if your partner seems preoccupied and is blocked over this, ask him or her to give you the thing he or she would most like to see you wearing when you come to lovemaking, and wear it. If you really can't share these essential kids' games or communicate such turn-ons for fear of each other's reactions, you shouldn't be in bed together at all. Noncommunication, not normal human fantasy, lands people in the divorce court for incompatibility; a fantasy which really turns you off is a subject for discussion and adjustment through make-believe, and, just as men tend to be programmed for concrete signals, women are programmed to pick up the kind of signal which turns their partner on – after a few big orgasms together, all but the oddest fantasies get to be shared.

So, if he likes you to look like a cross between a snake and a seal, wear what he gives you. If you like him a particular way, see he knows it. Some women are bothered that a man who occasionally likes them to dress him in their clothes is unvirile (it causes less anxiety the other way round). But all of us have a person of the opposite sex inside us – Queen Omphale dressed

clothes

*Undressing can be tender or it
can be rough; but whichever, it
should be skillful.*

the hero Hercules in her clothes, and he wasn't exactly unvirile.
This is a common game or ceremony in other cultures. We
accept sex as pleasure and are starting to accept it as play. Now
we need to accept it as ceremony, plus the fact that we are all
bisexual and that sex includes fantasy, self-image, psychodrama,
and the other things which our society still finds worrying. Bed
is the place to act these things out – that is one of the things
human sex is for. See *Playtime*.

Special preferences apart, it's worth knowing at least as
much as a pro about the common turn-ons, because for most
couples they have stunning surprise value as unscheduled
extras on special occasions. If a particular one doesn't work, you
needn't repeat it.

stockings

Can be a sex turn-on – often the preferred ones are old-style black stockings which look naughty. Panty hose are an obstacle unless crutchless, and only erotic, for most males, if worn without panties, and then chiefly visually. It is said that if you can get one stocking off her you're home. Actually in quick undressing or actual lovemaking both panty hose and stockings usually get ruined, but if you keep your nails and fingers smooth, taking them off gently makes good foreplay, along with mutual undressing generally. Long gloves turn some people on – they suggest the old-style great lady. Unless you find shoes sexy, lovemaking is best with bare feet and toes.

g-string

No longer confined to sex shops, these are now widely available. It should tightly cover the whole pussy and pubic hair, nothing else. It should undo from the sides with hooks, or better with ribbons, so that it can be taken off when astride without kicking your man. The traditional "leaf" worn by Japanese prostitutes is made of silk, not nylon, because it holds your perfume better. The sexiest g-string isn't street wear – you wear it only for sex: the first direct genital kiss is given, or taken, through it. Later you can surprise him by suddenly taking the two ends and puffing it hard over his nose and mouth. Men are catered for, with so-called "posing pouches" worn by would-be strong-men for near-nude photos. Use these in the same way.

Two such minimum g-strings make the ideal nightwear, if you want nightwear. For actual use in intercourse, as opposed to dressing up, it is best to make your own. White or black pure silk are the best materials. When on, it should be absolutely tight and skin smooth, covering the vulva and pubis. Cotton will do – nylon has the wrong texture. Other materials can be used as turn-ons, for looks, but can't really be kissed through – if you want to use these, wear them over the silk "leaf". Open-fronted panties aren't the same thing.

chastity belt

A turn-on for some people, they were once sold in earnest to "prevent masturbation". Like clothes, the real fun is in eventually taking them off. Many commercial ones don't even prevent intercourse. The kind with built-in stimulation, vibrators, and so on sound more fun but cost a bomb. The genuine article, as used in the thirteenth century, wasn't meant to lock up the woman, but was worn by her as a deterrent against rape – the woman usually had the key, and some

stockings
Seeing them on and taking them off are both consistent turns-on.

women were buried in them to prevent posthumous violation. The only worthwhile chastity-belt game is to try, when she has a period, how many ways you can circumvent a really tight g-string and both achieve orgasm. Male versions are sold and appeal to some people, presumably as a spinning-out technique. Expensive toys unless you want to make one.

shoes

A sex turn-on connected with the foot/pussy equivalence we've mentioned elsewhere (see *Feet*); symbols apart, it's interesting that shoe-leather "fixes" from sweat have exactly the same fatty acids that are present in the vagina and turn on male sex behavior in monkeys and apes. Though these smell rancid rather than sexy, they may still have a subliminal turn-on effect in man. High heels attract some males, chiefly for their effect in increasing the wobble in the female gait, another instance of making the woman more woman-shaped. Probably something of a hide-and-seek effect, too – Chinese women had to hide their feet, but could show their genitals.

For most lovemaking, you really need bare feet.

boots

Notorious sex turn-on for many people – the longer the better. Complicated symbolism here involving aggression (jackboots and so on), phallicism, and the female lower extremity. Used to be the badge of the prostitute – now general wear for everyone: have changed places with corsets, which used to be general wear and are now chiefly a sex kick. Odd how the market in the respectability of sexually symbolic clothing swings over the years. One could learn a lot about human imprinting by plotting the prevalence of such preferences.

Good for dressing-up games if you like them. Not very practical for serious sex unless you keep them for non-horizontal, non-bed activities. If your man likes them, try appearing suddenly in long, tight, black shiny ones.

corsets

A turn-on for some people – now generally confined to sex games; they used to be an obligatory article of fashion, and still make occasional appearances on the catwalk. Make a woman still more woman-shaped. Firm pressure on the waist and abdomen excites many women. Some men are turned on by being laced into them too. Probably work through tightness and skin pressure, but a lot of symbolisms are involved.

leather

Probably the most popular superskin turn-on: black hide also looks aggressive or scary, and, being skin, all leather fixes natural sex odors. Unlike rubber, you can wear it without being thought kinky, which is yet another example of the arbitrary social choice of sex turn-ons in clothing. Some men like women encased in it: those who like the ferocious buckled-up look don't go for wet-look, soft leather, and vice versa. If your partner likes it on you, let him or her do the buying. This is one object turn-on which women respond to as well as men, especially if it feels and smells right – soft leather jockstraps seem to please some people of both sexes. Don't pay racketeer prices, however; most of the elaborate gear in fetishistic toy-shops can be improvised, and Avengers-style suits are not that difficult to get hold of. See *Boots*, *Clothes*. Even if the texture doesn't appeal, try a leather-based (*cuir de Russie*) perfume – it is probably the closest to the normal female attractant odor.

rubber

This turns some people on, and is a wholetime fetish with others. Effect seems to depend on its status as superskin combined with tightness and odor. The odor of latex rubber excites a lot of people if they have come to associate it with using condoms – it also enhances the normal female perfume. Wash anything rubber in soapy water, dry, and keep in French chalk – this includes reusable condoms, ticklers, g-strings, and larger items. Black seems to be the preferred sexual color. The livid pink condoms sold in some places don't look as good as the normal translucent variety.

There was a time when rubber clothing was only seen in the context of skin-diving and water-skiing. Today, it's not unusual to find it on the high street.

In the slang sense, remember: for any sex act where there is either a lack of information or the slightest doubt, condoms are obligatory as an anti-HIV precaution. There should be no argument about this and no exceptions: no glove, no pussy.

ice

The last material one would consider sexy – yet we keep hearing of people who use it for its shock effect on the skin. One sex book suggests that just before orgasm the woman should slap a handful of crushed ice on her partner's back. Other people use an ice cube to go slowly over a partner's skin, including the soles of the feet, put them in each other's navels during sexual games, and so on. Not so strange, when you come to think of it – cold is a strong skin stimulus. We see no objection to experiments if you like the idea – you will hardly catch cold on one ice cube. Don't use super-cooled ice, let alone dry ice; these stick fast to moist surfaces and burn like a red-hot iron. Test any ice cube you use on your tongue, cautiously, otherwise you may be in for a shock.

wet look

Another superskin releaser – it makes you tight and shiny. Some people like the real thing with real water – try showering in a clinging cotton shift: this both feels and looks sexy. Transparent plastic raincoats worn over the bare skin do something for some wearers and spectators, and are a fairly common male turn-on. Ask, try it, or both.

masks

These excite some people: if this seems odd, remember that they are the oldest human device for getting mystical as well as sexual inspiration, by making the wearer menacing, other than themselves, and "possessed" by the mask, and by altering the body image through partial sensory deprivation. There are

boots
Good for dressing-up games, but not very practical in bed.

inflatable helmets on the market which accentuate this last effect. We find sex better without our head in a bag. Putting the woman's panties over the man's head, an old professional trick, works on quite a different basis (see *Clothes*). Masks, like corsets, were once a general fashion.

Don't fool around with plastic bags – these are dangerous and obstruct breathing.

equipment

The Austrian gymnastic professor Van Weck Erlen wrote a book in which, along with over 500 postures you draw lots to carry out, he advised a "sexuarium" complete with gymnastic mat and trapezes. For his sort of sex you'd need them.

The idea of a "sexuarium" complete with mirrors, red light, and black decor turns some people on – there are a good few 1930s palaces in Beverly Hills which have one. On a smaller scale one can fit out the basement. Our preference is for the bedroom, however, and the result needn't be embarrassing.

The bed is discussed later. The gymnastic mat idea isn't a bad one at all a really thick carpet (or carpet piece if you can't afford it wall to wall) is as good, with plenty of room to roll around. Some people favor stools for the bent-over positions, front and back: as one needs a bedroom stool, this can be chosen

equipment

Extras are fun, but superlative sex still depends on the right person and the right attitude.

masks
The oldest human device for getting sexual inspiration.

for the right height. A pile of hard square cushions is more suited for diversification. Two of the bed pillows will be hard, for use in bed – the cushions are for floor work. If you like big mirrors, these can be inside closet doors, or turn over to show a chaste decoration.

The best chair for intercourse is a fully upholstered one without arms. If you want to tie each other to it, check for size and convenience – if you only want it for straight intercourse, it is best padded all over: or have separate chairs for each. A ceiling mirror is fun, but expensive and obvious if you mind that. You need an adjacent bathroom and shower. The ordinary motel bedroom layout is excellent for all these things, except that they don't pick the chairs with an eye to coition.

Naturally it is exciting to set up a fantasy place for fantasy experiences, complete with your own light show, if you have the money and energy. What we don't want to do here is to give the impression that you really need this – you don't, any more than you need a dream kitchen to be a first-class chef. You need the bare minimum – privacy, heating, washing space, a bed, one

mirrors

They turn love into a viewing occasion without loss of privacy.

or two ordinary furniture surfaces, genitalia which work, love, and imagination.

If you want extras, these will depend on what you want to do. Acrobatic position-merchants like to have a step-stool (fixed down, so it isn't dangerous) or even a short ladder. Some people fancy a rocking chair. Old-style bordels went in for all manner of stage sets, but these were either for the obsessed or once-in-a-while settings for an extra kick, not permanencies. Colored room light is an extra which some people find rewarding – so are a Land camera and a tape-recorder. If you use extras of any sort, from cushions or vibrators to cameras, lubricants, ropes or g-strings, make sure they are at hand and don't have to be fetched. Have a cloth towel ready – paper tissues stick to the skin. But you don't need any of these things to have superlative sex, given the right person and the right attitude.

Probably the only advantage of a really private sex-room is that you can fill it with erotic pictures without eroticizing normal guest space, and entertain Auntie without her asking what those rings in the wall are for. But a slide projector works fine on any white wall or ceiling, and you'd be surprised how unobservant the uninitiated can be.

mirrors

These have always been an important part of sexual furniture in any bedroom not wholly devoted to sleeping. They turn love into a viewing occasion without loss of privacy and help the mise-en-point at a practical level. They also provide a turn-on by letting you see yourselves – he can see his own erection and movements without stopping. She may be turned on by seeing her own body, watching herself masturbate, seeing herself bound, or any of the other fantasies one can enact, so that both get viewer as well as participant pleasure. Those who don't like them, by contrast, say they spoil the shut-in, non-spectator feeling they need to appreciate sensation to the full, and make the bedroom less like a womb with twins in it and more like Tiffany's.

If you have never made love in front of a big mirror, try it. You really need more than one to enable both to see clearly without having to shift around. The exercise is worth it, not only for voyeur effect, but also to show you how unridiculous you look making love. Sex described in cold blood, like instructions on how to put up a deck chair, sounds undignified, but seen as one participates it is natural, attractive, and formally beautiful to a morale-boosting extent, even if you aren't beautiful figures. If there does come a time when it's better to feel than look, we haven't reached it yet, in middle age.

What you have on your premises is your business, but, if you want to entertain guests, have the mirrors inside cupboard doors or on a stand. With all the publicity given to the one-way variety some couples are inhibited by anything they can't walk behind.

Old-style brothels went in for rooms of a hundred mirrors. Expense apart, these may or may not work for you; 100 couples acting in unison may be your turn-on, or they may remind you of Red Square on May Day or a Roman orgy, rather than lovemaking.

voyeurs

Title to be kept for those who treat sex as a nonplaying, spectator sport. Any active player is likely to be fascinated to watch his game being played, provided the players are worth watching. Real couples are worth watching – the bored, semi-erected participants in blue movies seldom merit the trouble. Real human mating behavior is as interesting as that of the birds of the air and the beasts of the field and far more instructive. If you can watch others, do, unless it violates your sense of privacy.

We lose a lot in this society by not being in the habit of making love in company. If we did, fewer books such as this one would need to be written.

pornography

Name given to any sexual literature somebody is trying to suppress. Most normal people enjoy looking at sex books and reading sex fantasies, which is why abnormal people have to spend so much time and money suppressing them. The only drawback of the commercial stuff is that because it is based on fantasy, and often inexperienced fantasy at that, it's not much help with sex practice for real lovers. Depiction of any of the range of sex behaviors we've described helps people to visualize them, which is why this book is illustrated. Commercial porno stories, however, tend to be dull, repetitive, and a strain on credulity. Frankly antisocial fantasies about torture and so on worry legislators and others for fear they might induce idiots to imitate them, though it's equally possible that, by enabling not very bright people to fantasize their unacceptable needs vividly, they help to keep them from acting them out, but we continue to lack good enough evidence to settle the matter one way or another.

Straight couples can use "pornography" constructively in the exact proportion that it's well done, i.e. it describes feasible, acceptable, and pleasurable sex activities they'd enjoy, or fantasies which, though not feasible, turn them on. This is what literature in general does.

Many people find sex books a real help in raising the level of feeling to bedpoint. Use them as football enthusiasts use football books – even if the players in the story show superhuman shooting powers. It isn't true that only men are turned on by sexual literature: it is true that women are most turned on by it if it's written with sensitivity and an awareness of other than male feelings.

If you've got literary or artistic ability, use it to express your own fantasies to the full, for private use between you. Many respected writers and artists have done this, even if they didn't publish the results – at least, not under their own names. It's one way of dealing with the things you can't, or wouldn't wish, to do in fact – a kind of accessory to dreams and to play.

The idea of children getting hold of pornography terrifies some people. If it deals simply with normal lovemaking, this fear is probably not justified – young children are likely to be bored. The main objection lies in how badly most of the black market stuff is produced – some is enough to put adults off. Some adult fantasy material, if it's odd or cruel, could be actively frightening, though no more so than non-sex material such as newsreels or religious books. If you do see your children with pornography, remember far more harm would be caused by any uproar you make about it. For adolescents, it's probably innocuous unless they're obviously very disturbed over sex.

gadgets and gimmicks

The great exponents of this sort of hardware previously were the Japanese. Judging from travellers' tales, most ethnographic sex aids are used by men at the insistence of women; they must be unusually keen to please in order to bore through the glans and fit a "spritsail yard", like the Kayans, or insert pebbles under the skin of the penis itself like the Sumatrans. In softer cultures, such devices are external – chiefly rings which fit round the coronal groove, made of feathers (*palang unus* – Malaya), goats' eyelids sewn back to back (Patagonia), or little hair brushes. These things are in museums, or one would wonder if somebody was putting an impertinent ethnographer on. The remarkable thing is that they should stay in place during intercourse. Nearly all are damnably uncomfortable to wear, and either pinch or get caught with hairs.

European equivalents are warty condoms, rings, and the like, and dildoes – penis supplements or penis substitutes.

Sheaths are straightforward – they come in all manner of shapes and contours, the aim being to roughen both the penis and the vaginal barrel. Some have knobs or fingers to tickle the cervix. We are at a disadvantage here, in that these are supposed to help the female enjoy, but we've never yet met a woman who liked them. They are not safe contraceptives. Some people who are excited by the idea, if not by the sensation, buy a full set, including all the possible variations of shape. They come complete with a drying frame on which they can be stretched for cleaning, and should then be rolled and powdered with French chalk.

The kind with a thick corona ring strike us as downright painful. They also destroy the direct physical contact which, in communicative sex, matters a lot, but they allow one to experiment – such sexual Easter bonnets at least add novelty if you like the idea. We think they are more likely to precipitate frigidity than cure it, unless novelty is your turn-on. Buying sex gear together from a catalogue helps some people to fantasize and communicate.

Penis extensions, which fit over the real thing, likewise; penis size, it can't be repeated too often, has little to do with sexual feeling, though a big one may be emotionally stimulating in prospect. A large, hard extension can do actual damage. The most these do is to boost male morale, though, like a chest wig, one wouldn't like to be found using one.

Rings are another matter. These are basically erection-maintainers; where they work, they can be a real help to better intercourse by stiffening a part-erection after a full orgasm – this is achieved by slightly blocking off the veins of the penis at its root to keep the hydraulics working. At the same time, being worn over the pubis, they can also provide an additional pressure-point for the clitoris. The finest specimen we've seen is Chinese and made of ivory. The two sky-dragons are sporting with a pearl (the semen) – in use, the pearl is a small knob to fit the clitoris, the scales of the dragons open and tickle the labia, and the whole thing is held in place by a long tape passed through the hole, back between the legs, crossing behind the scrotum, up between the buttocks, and then round the waist.

The Chinese and Japanese also bind thin leather round the whole penis, or its base, and the Japanese favor openwork tubes fitting over the whole thing – in each case, pressure at the base plus roughening of the shaft and pubic area constitute the point. Others are belt-like devices which hold back the foreskin by pulling on the penile root. There are now several up-to-date models in rubber or plastic, which fit round the base of the shaft and have a clitoris tickler to supplement the man's pubic bone.

Quite a few of the clitoral knobs strike us as over-hard to be comfortable, and all rubber rings are apt to pinch one or other partner. We have yet to meet anyone, male or female, who got much out of them. None of these things is a surefire erection device, and most work at all only in the absence of any impotence anxieties. One, the Blakoe ring, goes round both penis and scrotum-root (it opens and clips shut), to maintain agreeable erotic sensations and hence boost morale. To stiffen erection, a ring needs to go round the roots of both penis and scrotum – some lovers use a turn of cord. Professionals and some good amateurs use it to produce elaborate "cockties" which compress the root, separate the testes, and hold the penis in a bent-double position, giving a sensation rather like continuous suction. One can buy assorted leather harnesses with similar effects. Don't bruise the urethra by over-tightening or leave on too long. Metal rings frequently have to be removed at Outpatients when they get stuck on an erection. One wearer, on his way to an assignation, set off an airport metal detector. He told officials it was an article of his religious faith.

Dildoes are artificial penises of varying sophistication (some include warmth and ejaculatory capacity, others built-in

This is about the most mind-blowing sexual sensation of which most males are capable.

vibrators). These go back to the most ancient times and presumably have takers – the modern ones have excellent texture. Most women do not naturally masturbate by vaginal insertion, but, since the ladies of the Turkish harem "were not suffered a radish or cucumber to their diet except it be first sliced," some, with sexual experience, evidently do – and the sight of a woman using one is clearly a turn-on for some males. They can also provide a second penis for simultaneous use. Single dildoes with a harness, or double-ended dildoes, are intended for woman–woman relations.

Merkins are vagina-substitutes – traditionally a warm-water container with a rubber or plastic vagina. Attached to an inflatable plastic doll or not, we doubt their utility – there is no substitute for what they attempt to replace, and, like the traditional hole in a watermelon, the only excuse for using them in two-way sex is if the sight of a merkin in use excites your partner. Vagina substitutes with a pump "to enlarge the penis," apart from bolstering the folklore about penile size, are capable of permanently damaging the natural hydraulics and should be avoided.

Chinese bells (now usually Japanese – *rin-no-tama*) are something else again. These are hollow ivory or plastic spheres, one empty, one containing mercury, and the third a large steel ball and a number of small metal tongues. They can either be inserted (in reverse order) into the vagina or put between the labia. Some are single, eggshaped devices. Movement, including walking, then produces a quite unique pelvic sensation more intermittent and intimate than a vibrator. Some can be used in actual intercourse, others to maintain a steady stimulation – all day, if you can take it. Follow the manufacturers' instructions.

Skin gloves and skin thimbles have appeared on the market, but good ones have yet to be made. These are far better worth trying than any of the gadgets mentioned so far, except for the Chinese bells. They consist either of a whole glove or, better, a series of finger-cots the size of a thimble, each covered with a bristly cloth ranging in texture from soft fur to hard nylon pile with a tuft of bristles where the nail would be on a finger. They are used for erotic massage of the skin in either sex. With a properly chosen range of bristles and some natural skill, these can produce an effect which ranges from the pleasant to the excruciating. A well-made set would make a fine personal present. See also *Vibrators, Japanese style, Pattes d'araignée*.

Our final judgment is that, unless intravaginal gadgets help the sexually disabled, which we doubt, they're a waste of good money. For most people, they only spoil the intensity of normal feeling. Skin stimulation is another matter. But we may be unusual.

Clothing which maintains continuous sexual excitement is an old human expedient, and well worth experimenting with. Most of it is designed for women, not out of male chauvinism but simply because of the difference in physiology: a continuous turn-on enhances the woman's eventual response but would tend to overload the man's and make him unable to perform.

The traditional instances are geared to feel sexy for the wearer and look sexy to her partner. Some of them could be of real use in relearning the proper sexual use of our skin. They range from long heavy earrings to tight straps, corsets and belts, rough textures (hair shirts, bamboo-ring shirts), ankle chains, footwear which affects the gait and presses on the instep, and now, more explicitly, hot pants which fit well into the vulva. See the full history of such devices in Bernard Rudofsky's *The Unfashionable Human Body*.

Most turn women on by their skin and muscle effect and men by their symbolism, but some couples get a special kick if she wears something wild under ordinary clothes on social occasions, when one can't go home early. Some commercial ones lock, and you leave the key at home. Could be worth trying for men too, if only in the interest of fair shares. Continuous sexual excitement you can't stop or do anything about would at least make a dull occasion more interesting, and guarantee a good scene when you finally get home. See *Earrings, Gadgets and gimmicks, Jokes and follies*.

slow masturbation

Prostitutes aren't usually much good at advanced sex: this is about the one old-time bordel trick which is worth trying. To make it work, you need to know how to tie your partner (see *Bondage*) and to have a partner who likes struggling against resistance, but it works for a great many people. Traditionally, the woman does it to the man, but it works in either direction. You need good access and a completely helpless partner, though you can try it without if bondage games turn you off, but the result is quite different and you can't get so far. The knack lies in playing on your partner like an instrument, alternately pushing them forward and frustrating them (compare *Relaxation*).

The woman starts by tying the man to her satisfaction, either staked out, or wrists behind and ankles crossed, knees open, naked, and on his back. She then "signs her name" (*le coup de cassolette*). To do this, she kneels astride him, facing him, and performs a tasteful striptease as far as her panties. Next, holding his hair in her hand, she rubs his mouth firmly over her armpit and breasts, giving him her body perfume. Then she locks her legs carefully round his neck and presses her covered pussy on his mouth. Finally, she strips off and gives him the direct genital kiss, (brushing first, then open, taking her time over it), pulls his foreskin well back if he has one, and stands back for a few moments to let him get excited. If she knows her job, he will be unable to move, while the kiss ensures that he won't lose the feel of her. Coming back, she does the same all over again, stiffens him by hand and mouth if necessary, and starts in real earnest.

She has two focal points to attend to, his mouth and his penis, and the knack, during this warm-up period, consists in keeping both of them occupied continuously, without pauses and without triggering ejaculation. The possibilities are obvious – hand to each, hand to one, mouth or pussy to the other; varied by a touch of her breasts, her armpit, or even her hair. Between the two poles, she will work over his most sensitive areas with her fingertips (*les pattes d'araignée*), her tongue, and her pussy – this last with one hand on his penis and her other palm over his mouth, never letting the rhythm slacken. If his erection begins to go down, she stops, tightens him up (this is the moment for thumb-tying if she is strong enough to turn him easily), then re-stiffens him. Then she can begin slow masturbation proper.

This is about the most mind-blowing (and, while it lasts, frustrating) sexual sensation of which most males are capable. (If you still want to know why we say start by tying your lover, try it for a few moments with an unbound partner.) Sit well up on his chest, with your buttocks to his chin, and put each of your ankles inside the crook of one of his knees. Hold the root of his penis with one hand and with the other pull the skin back as far as it will go with finger and thumb, thumb toward you. Then start quick, sharp, nervous strokes – each one quick, that is, but timed at one per second, no faster. After about 20 of these, give about 10 very quick strokes. Then resume the slow rhythm. And so on. If from the turmoil under you and the general scene you think he is about to ejaculate, drop the speed (you can sense this with practice). Keep it up as long as you think he can stand it. The excitement is his, but is less one-sided than it sounds; the male response is enough to turn most women on, and you can press your open pussy hard on his breastbone, but don't let your attention wander. Ten minutes is about as much as most males can stand. If he goes limp, put him out of his misery, either by quickly masturbating him to climax, or by mouth, or by turning and riding him. When he does come, get him untied as quickly as possible – delay after orgasm will leave him as stiff as if he'd played a hard ball-game.

This is the Japanese-massage-special-treatment routine – the only bar to making it at home, like sukiyaki, is if you are a big girl. The Japanese are artists at making their knots, like their dishes, look really nice, and Japanese masseuses are small enough to sit on a man's chest without killing him. If you are large, try tying his legs apart and taking your weight on your knees, with your pussy on his mouth: in the story of Brunnhilde, she tied up King Gunther on his wedding night, probably for a similar routine – we've given the small woman version. Let him try the same techniques on you.

The man has three points to concentrate on – mouth, breasts, and clitoris. A fairly tight couple of turns round the breasts helps (careful!). He can start as she did, with the *coup de cassolette* (armpit and glans) and then rub his hand over her *cassolette* and put it over her mouth, to play back her own perfume.

He needs to watch from her sounds and movements how heavy a touch on the clitoris she can stand. He can copy the spinning-out technique and excite her by postponement, but usually he will get better results by simply pushing her as far and as fast as possible. If she is a responsive subject and not frightened of the whole business, the reaction will fully test his skill in securing her. He should kneel astride, but not sit on her, nor hold her down – she should be quite helpless anyway. Finally, and with experienced lovers this will be when she is semi-conscious, he will switch to a few moments of tongue work for lubrication, then vigorous intercourse, and make her scale another, still higher range of peaks, taking his own orgasm early on. He should know by the feel of her when to stop – this bears no relation to mewing and struggles, which reach a peak just short of climax. He should then untie her quickly, skillfully, and painlessly, so that she comes back to earth lying quietly in his arms.

One unexpected trick is for the woman to tell her partner she's going to give him the time of his life, tie him, and then, when you've made sure he can't get loose or make a sound, make him watch while you masturbate to orgasm. This is more exciting for both of you than it sounds. He, if he's already excited and expecting something else, will go beserk, and his useless struggles will turn her on. Afterwards she can make it up to him – slowly.

bondage

Bondage, or as the French call it, *ligottage*, is the gentle art of tying up your sex partner – not to overcome reluctance, but to boost orgasm – and the second most popular sexual fantasy (after group sex). It's one unscheduled sex technique which a lot of people find extremely exciting, but until recently were scared to try, and a venerable human resource for increasing sexual feeling, partly because it's a harmless expression of sexual aggression – something we badly need, our culture being very uptight about it – and still more because of its physical effects: a slow orgasm when unable to move is a mind-blowing experience for anyone not too frightened of their own aggressive self to try it.

"Any restraint upon muscular and emotional activity generally," wrote Havelock Ellis, "tends to heighten the state of sexual excitement." Men and women have always been excited anyhow by the idea of getting the better of each other, and "erotic bondage" was always a popular turn-on – every self-respecting folk-heroine and most folk-heroes have to be bound hand and foot periodically so they can be rescued. The best man at a Berber wedding ties up the bride if she struggles, and she is expected to struggle so she can be tied up. Fantasies of the same sort have a big written and pornopicture literature (most of it wildly unpracticable and meant to be seen not felt) which acts as a substitute for people who are hung up on aggression, or need an illusion of rape to be able to lie back and enjoy without guilt. Most of us have traces of these needs, and like to "dominate" each other symbolically at times, or be dominated (no offense to anyone's sexual politics, because this need is mutual). But bondage games are played by many straight lovers who want kicks, not substitutes, and fill a lot of important spaces. They take a little learning (first efforts are often painful, or come adrift, or waste an erection messing around) but with speed and skill many unlikely people swear by them as an occasional – if only because really professional slow masturbation isn't possible unless the subject is securely tied.

Many women enjoy the helplessness and temporary exaggeration of male control, but bondage is an even better dodge for her to use on the over-macho male: he gets the mind-blowing sensation of "becoming one enormous penis", plus withdrawal of all performance anxiety – she gets the opportunity to be in total control of the pace and character of arousal, possibly for the first time. Part of the current popularity of this kind of sexual play lies in exorcizing each partner's fear of control by the other by turning it into a source of increased physical sensation. Each enjoys the other's pretend fierceness. Porno bondage literature is good on technique, but off-putting by playing up male hostility, which doesn't fit in the real enactment: psychiatric books, when aware of it, lump it in with sadomasochism. It could, of course, be played in that way, as can sex in general: the best guarantee that it won't be is strict insistence on equal turns.

In fact, really skillful bondage works like a bomb, sexually, on most non-timid males, both on the giving and the receiving end (as with any trick which involves both stimulation and symbolism, a well-tied sexual "prisoner" both looks and feels sexy) – and on a fair proportion of women once they get the idea; eventual responders of both sexes can require a lot of gentle preparation if they are scared by the aggressive symbolism, but this kind of fantasy only frightens people whose idea of tenderness is over-tender. Some women sense the need to be "overpowered" sometimes. Others are into the domination symbol and like to be aggressors from the start. The idea is to tie your partner hand and foot, firmly but comfortably, so that they can struggle as hard as they like without getting loose, and then bring them to orgasm. Apart from being a wild sexual sensation, it enables many people who can't otherwise do so to let go to the last degree. They may yell blue murder at the critical moment, but love it (one important skill here is to distinguish the noises which mean real distress – kinked wrists, cramp, or the like – from the normal protests of ecstasy: the first mean "stop at once," the second "for God's sake go on and finish me off").

Games of this sort are an occasional optional extra to all sorts of sex-play and intercourse, since the tied partner can be kissed, masturbated, ridden, or simply teased to orgasm, but they go extra-well in both sexes with the unbearably sharp sensations produced by slow, skillful handwork. "Restraint" gives the receiving partner something muscular to do while remaining quite helpless to influence the march of events, or the rhythm and speed of stimulation (what Theodor Reik called the "suspense factor"), and enables the active partner to push the woman, at least, to unbearable lengths (she, when her turn comes, can drive him frantic by spinning things out).

To make this work as a game, it obviously needs to be effective, but not painful or dangerous. Technique is worth a few words because this is a highly popular sex fantasy, and some skill and care are called for. On any bed with four posts, you can stake a partner out, supported by one or more pillows. This is the traditional bordel method, probably because it needs no skill. Extension like this inhibits orgasm in some people – many feel more with the legs open, but the wrists and elbows firmly behind the back, or by being tied to a chair, or upright to a post. The critical areas where compression boosts sex feeling are the wrists, ankles, elbows (don't try to make them meet behind by brute force), soles of the feet, thumbs, and big toes (artful women break off halfway to tie these last two with a leather bootlace – if you doubt this, try it).

There are divergences of taste over what to use for tying. Leaving aside kinks like straitjackets or boy-scout garters, different couples use leather or rubber straps, ribbons, cloth strips, pyjama cords, or thick, soft rope. Straps are easiest for those who aren't very strong or can't tie reef knots. They need holes at half-inch intervals. Triangular bandages are all right for quick hand-and-foot tying, but don't look very sexy – and it is the neatness and wriggling of the parcel which excite the active party. Old stockings are a favorite resource, but murder to untie quickly in an emergency. Chains, handcuffs, and so on are quick, but don't give any compression and hurt to lie on. If they lock, you can't rely on releasing them quickly. The weird aparatus sold by adult-toy-makers is for the birds unless you only want to pose for photographs. If you like it, make your own. For most couples, a hank of cotton clothesline is fine. Cut it into five or six four-foot and a couple of six-foot lengths, and use a lot of hand-tight turns – don't tie tight enough to bruise. Put it through the washing machine with softener before use.

Some energetic people like to be gagged as well. As one lady put it, "it keeps the bubbles in the champagne." Gagging and being gagged turns most men on – most women profess to hate it in prospect, but the expression of erotic astonishment on the face of a well-gagged woman when she finds she can only mew is irresistible to most men. Apart from the symbolism and the "feeling of helplessness" it enables the subject to yell and bite during orgasm, which helps a total cut-loose, unless you have a rhinoceros hide and live in a soundproof room. It makes prompting impossible, so that your partner's initiatives are outside your control. Most men who are excited by this sort of game like to be silenced thoroughly. Untimid women often come to like it after a few tries if they're the biting kind or like the feeling of helplessness – others hate it and lose their orgasm if they try it. A few like to be blindfolded as well, or instead.

It's actually hard to gag anyone 100 percent safely, except in movies, where a wisp of silk over the heroine's face enables the

hero to walk past without hearing her. This is as well, as the
prisoner must never be made incapable of signalling if anything
is wrong. A long piece of cloth, with several turns well between
the teeth, or a small rubber ball fixed in the middle of a one-
inch strap by a nut and bolt (the *poire* of French bordel tradition)
are quite fierce enough. Adhesive tape will silence someone, but
is torture to take off. Anything in the mouth must be firm,
mustn't block breathing, and must be quick-release in case the
subject signals danger – from choking, feeling sick, or any other
source of discomfort. This signal (and this goes for all bondage
games) must be agreed beforehand and never abused or
ignored – penalty for illicit use, two further orgasms. A Morse-
code grunt, "shave and a haircut, two bits", is a safe choice. The
Federal Safety Code must be observed and displayed in a
prominent place on the premises. This is as follows:

1 Nothing may ever be tied round the front of anybody's neck,
however loosely, and even if they ask for it.

2 Nothing loose or soft, which can get into the throat, or in
general other than we've specified, may be put in anyone's
mouth, or over their face. All gags or knots must be quick-release.

3 Nobody helpless may ever be left alone, even briefly,
especially face-down or on a soft surface like a bed. Don't leave
a partner tied and go to sleep, especially if either of you have
been drinking. Don't keep anyone tied up for longer than half
an hour.

4 Play bondage games only with people you know, not only
socially but also sexually, never with acquaintances, and avoid
group scenes. This goes for couples as well as partners – some
people are careless, and others are sadists.

Apart from this, cruelty of any sort, tying someone who is really
scared of the idea, tight cords, stuffing things in people's
mouths, idiot tricks like hanging people up by any part of their
anatomy, and the whole Sadie-Mae routine, which to most
couples is simply painful and a turn-off, belong to
psychopathology, not lovemaking. Bondage as a pleasurable sex
game is never painful or dangerous. It can, of course, be played
simply for the symbolic aggression, but at least half the payoff
in people (and there are many) who enjoy it is, for the person
tied, directly physical, in struggling against restraint and in skin
and muscle feeling, plus the release of any surviving childhood
blocks which comes from having pleasure "administered" willy
nilly. It also helps get over our cultural taboo on intense
extragenital sensations, which belongs in the same package.

Ropemarks usually go in a few hours if you've been gentle.
Rope burns and bruises come from clumsy untying – don't saw
through the skin, but be quick, so that the man doesn't get stiff
through being left tied after orgasm, and the woman comes
down to earth lying comfortably in your arms. You can be

agreeably, adequately, and symbolically fierce, whichever your sex, without being spiteful or clumsy and wrecking things.

The right mix here, as in all sex games, is tough plus tender. If you can't sense how tough your partner likes it, ask, then subtract 20 percent to allow for the difference between fact and fantasy. Given these rules, any couple who enjoy violent lovemaking and like the idea could do worse than learn to make each other helpless occasionally, gently, quickly, and efficiently. This is neither kinky nor frightening – just human. For the *pièce de résistance* which goes with bondage, namely *Slow masturbation*, see that section.

harness

Quick "restraint" system for people who can't tie knots, bruise with rope, or like the look of "apparatus". Comes in all degrees of complication and for all postures – watch out for expensive confections which are really kinky-photo props. Mainstay of fetish boutiques. Includes some gadgets like the mono-glove which holds the elbows back without cutting into the arms. Gives very tight restraint and a lot of skin pressure, which some people favor. Some play up the horse-symbolism, or include chastity belts, corsets, etc.

chains

The tied-up, tinkling look – they show well on naked skin. Some women like both the coldness and the symbolism, and some men spend hours locking and unlocking them – you could try them on him too for size. Uncomfortable and only symbolically effective if you want actually to hold a partner still, but they look fierce, and some people find them exciting. Bright tinkling objects turn on magpies as well as people. See *Earlobes*.

vibrators

These are no longer an embarassing aid for the lonely or inexperienced. There are two main kinds – penis-shaped, which can be used on skin, breasts, clitoris, or deeply in the vagina (the small size can be used anally), and larger motor-driven kinds as used by masseurs, which strap on the hand like a glove, and can impart wild sensations to almost any part of the body. Vibrators are no substitute for a penis – some women prefer them to a finger for masturbation, or put one in the vagina while working manually on the clitoris. Lovers often find them an extra sensation to incorporate into the ritual of

discipline

Skin stimulation and the occasional spank at the right moment fit well into most people's repertoire.

skin stimulation. Vibrating hotel beds, operated by a coin-in-slot timer, are also well spoken of, but are apt to run out at the critical moment, or make you ill. Careful vibratory massage of the whole body surface is a better bet than over-concentration on the penis or clitoris, but it requires skill. Penile gadgets of various kinds for attachment to the standard vibrator base don't seem to have much beyond novelty to commend them.

discipline

Codeword for beating each other as a sexual technique. There is a venerable superstition, starting among English private-school scholars and backed by a vast literature from Meibom's *De Usu Flagrorum*, that beating is a sort of sexual Tabasco, the hottest erotic condiment, and no wild party and no wide-scope porn is complete without it. Some of this is due to the fact that specialists in this field haven't suffered under the handicaps that affected, say, *soixante-neuf* or straight sex – beating is decent and can even be done in church; sex isn't.

Beating is a kick which either works or doesn't. It doesn't work on either of us, so here we speak from inexperience. It's a violent skin stimulus, and Freud has been fully into the symbolism of punishment which goes with this – his conclusions go a long way to complicate Skinnerian arguments over what stimuli are "aversive" and which act as rewards. Quite apart from fantasists and talkers who are far more excited by the idea than the actual performance, some people are wildly turned on by it. For others, who have a real problem here, it may be necessary as a self-starter. Skin stimulation and the occasional spank at the right moment fit well into most people's repertoire. Most find that anything more is disappointing in proportion to the scale of the performance (and possibly conducive to the thoroughly erroneous idea that women, in particular, enjoy being beaten up). If you are lovers and one of you wants to be on the receiving end, the other need not be scared that they'll let out the beast in themselves by co-operating. If one of you wants to beat the other and he or she doesn't like it, or is turned off by the idea, that's harder – probably the loving answer is to settle for a lot of let's pretend and not much actual beating. This is a clear case where, if you can't communicate fantasies, you shouldn't be lovers. Play it through a few times in words during straight intercourse (see *Birdsong at morning*). When you try it in practice, if it's the ritual which is the exciting part, make that big – don't be ashamed to ask for this, or give it: play matters. It can be a naughty child or a mistress-and-slave routine or whatever – if your partner's fantasy doesn't turn you on naturally, play it as a game and enjoy his or her response. If it's the physical sensation, rhythm and style apparently matter far more than force.

Start gently at around one blow in one or two seconds, not more; gradually build up force until it is enough to make your subject want and not want you to stop. For two-way traffic, the result, plus struggling, should both look and feel sexy, not cruel. The sauna twig level is nearly enough for most couples, but people who really go for beating like it hard enough to mark the skin. You can stick to the buttocks or cover the whole surface – back, belly, breasts, and even penis (careful!) and vulva (put her on her back with her feet attached to the bedposts above her head, legs wide open; start on the buttocks, then give one light switch or two upon her thighs and vulva to finish her off). Or tie the victim hands over head to the shower nozzle and work over them under running water. For a genuinely decadent European sensation, you need real birch twigs. Canoe birch and gray birch, which are the nearest U.S. species, don't grow in the West, so if you live in California and want authenticity you may have to vacation with a chainsaw in the East or in Canada. You cut 2- to 3-foot straight branches with the twigs before the leaves come out, tie them into a bunch, and wet them before use. If you prefer all the trappings, one can buy ferocious-looking whips and paddles that make a great noise, but do no mischief. People who want the physical stimulus usually prefer twigs. Don't use bamboo – it cuts like a knife. Don't play this game with strangers, ever. Lovers have enough feedback not to let the most violent play go sour. And never mix purely erotic beating with real anger or bad temper – it could be dangerous. A game is a game is a game.

foursomes and moresomes

Uninhibited sex with multiple partners, often anonymous, which is the commonest of private fantasies and became realizable at the height of the era of sexual experimentation, is no longer possible because of the AIDS epidemic. There is no reason, however, why stable couples should not make love in each other's company. That can be liberating or disruptive, and in either case the motives and complications involved are not usually fully comprehensible to the parties involved. There is something to be said for anything which breaks down either the numbing convention of sexual privacy or the equally numbing convention of possessiveness, but the psychological hazards are considerable for any but very secure people.

The occasional, promiscuous sex which characterized the Californian "open sexuality" cult of the 1960s and 1970s was based on a structured, temporary suspension of social inhibitions. Predictably, in California, it was apt to become an addictive lifestyle. It had observable psychological effects on participants, both beneficial and destructive. Since it would now be suicidal, the argument is academic for the duration of the AIDS epidemic: the anonymous type of exchange cultivated by swingers and orgiasts of the early 1970s is much too dangerous. This applies to any sexual exchange with unknown quantities, dark horses, or couples who have slept around extensively, particularly if it involves any male–male bisexual experiences, or people who have had such experiences. It's hard enough to check the record of your own partner without checking that of another couple, emotional repercussions aside.

This doesn't apply to the sharing of sexual experience by enjoying it in company, particularly if we were able to approach this in the spirit of religious experience rather than of kicks. Religious promiscuity in the Tantrik and Vallabhacharya sects had a totally different object. Partners were assigned at random to remove any affectional element: the partners were to be not I and Thou, but the God and the Goddess, and the object was not sensory or emotional kicks, but the prolongation of the phase of pre-orgasm, normally brief, to use it as a launch pad for mystical experience, the putting together of Adam and Eve to form the Paradisal apple. It's perhaps more relevant for moderns in a non-mystical culture to point out that women not infrequently experience bodilessness and oceanic states in orgasm, though they may not make philosophical use of them – the problem would be to induce similar feelings in the male. This could become a project for two lovers with the woman, as is traditional, being the initiatrix. It doesn't need an "orgy", the novelty of which would be unhelpful in our culture even if it weren't, now, dangerous.

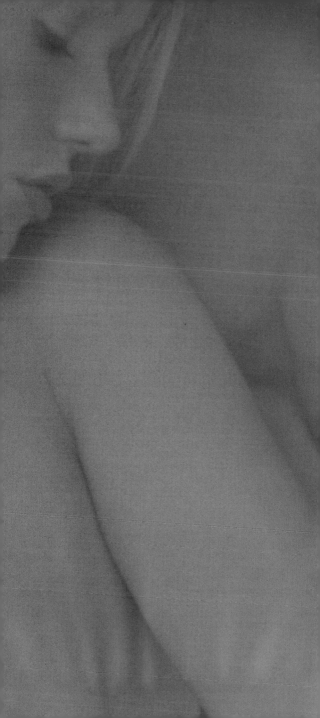

venues

beds

Still the most important piece of domestic sexual equipment. Really enthusiastic sex usually involves at one time or another almost every piece of furniture in the house, at least experimentally, but the bed is its commonest venue. Most beds on the market are designed by people who think they are intended to sleep on. The problem arises from the fact that the ideal surface for most kinds of intercourse needs to be rather harder than is comfortable for a whole night's sleep. One solution is to have two beds, one for sex and the other for sleeping, but this is a counsel of luxury, and in any case the need to move disrupts the best part of the night, the total relaxation which follows complete love. The best advice is probably to settle for a compromise and have a mattress on the floor as well. Enormous or circular beds look suggestive, but have no real advantages over a full-size double bed.

There are a few points we would consider before giving a seal of approval. First, since one uses the sides as well as the surface, the height needs to be right. The top of the mattress should be exactly level with the man's pubic bone – then, if you put your partner on or over it, she will be at the right height from in front or from behind. For some operations, especially bondage scenes if you like them, bedposts are essential, preferably tall ones, like those which hold up the canopies of antique beds, but not, for choice, a footboard, as you may want to use the end edge to start with, moving directly to full-length. Massive old bedframes have great advantages, in that they don't rattle or collapse. The mattress needs to be as hard as you can tolerate for comfortable sleep. Anything less forfeits the chief sexual joy of living and sleeping together – the fact that you can take one another at any hour of the night when both want it, and relax together immediately afterwards. If you have room, have a single bed as well, in case either partner is sick and feels more comfortable solo – twin beds have no place in a full sexual relationship.

Beside the bed itself you need four pillows – two very hard to go under the buttocks, and two soft, to sleep on. The room must be warm at all times of the year – warm enough to sleep without getting chilled – and without bedclothes if you wish. Electric blankets shouldn't therefore be necessary – the sort you lie upon will in any case not stand up to sexual intercourse. Unless you are very prosperous and it excites you to set up a special "sex room", bedroom chairs and stools can be chosen without too much ostentation to complete the necessary equipment for all eventualities (see *Equipment*), together with a soft rug, soft enough to be really comfortable for the underneath party, and mirrors. You also need enough bedside drawers to hold extras which you may need on impulse without having to get up and find them – lubricants, contraceptives, vibrators, and so on. A well-designed bedroom can be a sexual gymnasium without it being embarrassing to let elderly relatives leave their coats there.

Water beds can indeed produce extraordinary sensations, and they have a natural period of resonance which tends to take over – one has to move in their rhythm, but this itself is a stimulating constraint. Expensive – best kept for the odd extramural occasion when you re-honeymoon in a hotel room that's fitted with one. With the spread of inflatables, we may see a whole range of new sexual furniture-surfaces.

beds

The chief sexual joy of sleeping together is that you can take one another at any hour of the night.

quickies
*The rule is never to resist
linkup if it can be made
possible.*

quickies

Short and sharp has a charm of its own, but it needs a rate of mutual turn-on and physical response in the woman which is learned as a rule only in much longer sessions. A really good couple can manage either at will – short and sweet, or indefinitely prolonged and differently sweet. In other words, you can't fully appreciate the quickie without mastering the art of prolongation.

Once you've got this, the quickie is the equivalent of inspiration, and you should let it strike lightning fashion, any time and almost anywhere, from bed in the middle of the night to halfway up a spiral stair: anywhere that you're suddenly alone and the inspiration is bilateral. Not that one or other won't sometimes specifically ask, but the inspirational quickie is mutual, and half the fun is that the preliminary communication is wordless between real lovers. The rule is never to resist this link-up if it's at all possible – with quickness, wit, and skill, it usually is. This means proficiency in handling sitting, standing and other postures, and making love without undressing.

The ideal quickie position, the nude matrimonial, will often be out. This may mean you have to do it on a chair, against a tree, in a washroom. If you have to wait and can go straight home, it will keep up to half an hour. Longer than that and it's a new occasion. Around the house, try not to block, even if you are busy.

bathing

Bathing together is a natural concomitant of sex and a splendid overture or tailpiece. Taking an ordinary bath together has a charm of its own, though someone has to lean against the plumbing. Soaping one another all over, and, of course, drying one another, is a "skin game" which leads on naturally to better things; after intercourse, a bath together is a natural come-back to domesticity or work. There are now large baths and conversation baths, but most of us see them only in expense account hotels.

Actual coitus is possible, and fun, in the shower if your heights match (see *Showerbath*) but no ordinary domestic or hotel bath is big enough for intercourse without punishing your elbows. Beside the novelty, there isn't too much point anyway.

Sex while bathing is a different matter. The whole idea of intercourse in water is that it's like weightlessness or flying – the woman who is too big for all those Hindu climbing and standing postures becomes light enough to handle, and one can prop her at angles no acrobat could hold. All this was rediscovered in the California swimming pool era; when we get to the design of the future, indoor equivalents will certainly spread among non-millionaires. Meanwhile there is the sea, after dark, when it is warm enough – on a gradually shelving beach one can have enough privacy even by day, and even re-emerge clothed: spectators will take it for calisthenics or lifesaving. A pool has extras like steps and handholds, but is usually chlorinated.

Water doesn't hinder friction, though its relative chill may mean that it takes some brisk rubbing to get an erection even in a very eager male. It might be a good idea to insert before going in, if possible, or for the girl to wear a diaphragm – we haven't heard of any harm coming from being pumped full of seawater, but chlorinated pool water might just possibly be irritant, as it is to the eyes. You can have excellent straight intercourse lying in the surf if you can get a beach to yourselves, but sand is a problem, and keeps appearing for days afterwards. A floating mattress is effectively a waterbed, but it is hard to stay on it without concentrating.

We've heard of people combining coitus with swimming, and even scuba-diving, but they gave no practical details. Underwater coition, if more than a token contact, would use up vast amounts of air because of the overbreathing which goes with orgasm.

showerbath

Natural venue for sexual adventures – wash together, make love together: only convenient overhead point in most apartments or hotel rooms to attach a partner's hands. Don't pull down the fixture, however – it isn't weightbearing. See *Discipline*.

bathing
Soaping one another all over leads on naturally to better things.

jokes and follies

This, contrary to cultural traditions among prudes, is preeminently the right place for them. The best jokes, too, tend for this reason to be at their expense. The finger-raising quality of lovers vis-á-vis society is as necessary psychologically as their tenderness to each other. That, and not just the spice of danger, is what makes love in odd places and under other people's unperceptive noses so attractive. This is childish, but if you haven't yet learned to be childish in your lovemaking you should go home and learn, because it's important.

One mustn't let the joke go wrong and sour things: if you can have intercourse in a public restaurant or on Auntie's dining table and bring it off, you can laugh about it after (but if you don't bring it off you'll be lucky if you speak to each other again). Most couples contain, for any given occasion, one danger lover and one restraining influence, and achieve accordingly a commonsense balance, helped by the angel who watches over such lunatic antics and protects lovers from the consequences. All in all, it would be stupid to recommend them, but a pity to have missed them.

The amount of laughter you have in intercourse, pranks apart, is a measure, we think, of how well you are managing to love. It's evidence for, not against, the seriousness of your communication. If you have this, the laughs never fail, because sex is funny. If you haven't, you end with boxed ears, or tears, or no orgasm all round, through some remark "destroying the atmosphere". When it's really going, laughter is part of the atmosphere – even mockery isn't unaffectionate, and there's no joke like love well and mutually completed under unlikely circumstances. It's one of the few contemporary occasions which gets a laugh out of pure joy.

Taking a partner (usually female) around to social occasions nude, or in some kinky gear, under a long coat, is a danger-plus-snook-cocking game which some couples relish. The danger is there all right – if you must do it, make sure she really enjoys it. The no-panties bit is on the whole dangerous enough for most women unless it's very much their thing.

open air

Countries with a warm summer have advantages which can't be overstated. In England, to have regular and full love out of doors you need to be frostproof and own a park. In Ireland or Spain, even though it is warm in Spain, you need to be priest-proof as well. Most parts of the U.S. should count their blessings in this regard. What is odd is that they don't do more about garden design. The walled or hedged gardens of Europe are nearly all practicable, at least by night.

Outdoor locations in wild areas are often flawed by vermin, ranging from ants and mosquitos, to snakes and officious cops.

open air

Enthusiastic larks, like stripping right off, call for very remote areas or a walled garden.

Surface-wise the best venue is often sand dunes, which give shelter and keep the heat, besides not harboring stinging insects. Lawn grass is fine if well screened. The safest cover, if you intend to strip right off, is the thicket standing on its own, where you can see out, but they can't see in, the "bower" of Fontainebleau painters. Europeans, who live in crowded landscapes, are adept at quick dressing and using places like Hampstead Heath and the Prater.

With so much landscape to choose from, there should be no problem – if you do take risks, however, cultivate the quick getaway and the weather-eye open; danger turns some people on, and others, of both sexes, right off. Enthusiastic larks one gets lost in, like stripping right off or tying each other to trees, call for very remote areas or a walled garden.

What you can do safely in Hyde Park, London, would be asking for trouble in Central Park, New York. When traveling, Catholic countries are more uptight than Protestant, and nowhere is it desirable to offend local feeling. A flat roof at night is a standard Eastern venue – you can make love and see the whole city.

swings

These are one erotic extra which emphatically do work. Swinging solo can give many women an orgasm, because the acceleration produces pressure in the pelvis like nothing else.

Swings are of two sorts – those mentioned by Eastern writers are simply suspended garden-seat beds, not capable of this kind of acceleration, but giving the agreeable feelings that go with a slightly unstable surface, the proverbial jelly-on-springs. For him, this is like having a woman with infinite buttocks, for her it is a swimmy sensation, devoid of the drawbacks of an over-soft mattress, since the actual surface can be firm.

The real high-velocity swing is the woman's turn-on unless she gets air-sick first. The operative thing is the swoop, the falling-elevator sensation of negative G force. Swinging with a well-implanted partner is a sensation every woman should have at least once in a lifetime: solo swinging with the Japanese *rin-no-tama* (see *Gadgets and gimmicks*) is another wild experience of inner movement. A plastic egg-shaped saltshaker containing a really large ball bearing will do at a pinch.

For intercourse, he sits on the seat, and she astride facing – he works the swing, or a third party pushes (traditionally the maidservant). Ideally one should try the roller coaster, but we haven't found a showground which permits that. On a garden swing, watch out for the woman whose orgasm under these conditions is so intense that she blacks out, even if she doesn't do so normally, as she may fall if you don't hold her. Start at rest and penetrated, and use the movements of working up the swing to drive your coitus.

rocking chair

Tried by some as an indoor substitute for that classic piece of
sexual gear, the swing. Actually it feels quite different, lacking
the sudden belly dropping acceleration – the source of the
swing's effects on women – but more like the sensation of love
in a train (see *Railways*).

It works best with an ill-made chair on a very hard, rough
floor – better, an erotic rocking chair with a dozen flats or studs
on each rocker, hard cushions, and no arms. This still needs a
hard, preferably stone, floor and is infernally noisy – useless for
an apartment if people live under. Normally you sit astride
facing, but other positions are possible. We've seen a stool with
a powerful vibrator in the top cushion which looks worth a
trial, though the feel would be quite different.

railways

An old and favored site for "different" sex – now going out as
they abolish the old-style compartments. Whether it's the
motion and acceleration or the association with love on the run
that provides the turn-on isn't clear: it used to be fashionable in
the classier Parisian and Viennese bordels to have a
compartment fitted up, complete with train effects and noises,
and vibrated by a motor and cams. Since it is probably the
motion and variable G which score, choose a hard couch and a
winding track with numerous intersections and switches. In
emergency, there is just room for an upright in the washroom.

motorcars

These approach our ideal form of locomotion, the "double bed
with an outboard motor". Big American cars come very close to
it (there is room to lie flat, even on the rear seat). Compacts call
for neat handling of anything more than breast-and-petting
work. The classical postures (she on the back seat, he kneeling
between her legs, or both sitting, her legs round his waist) were
developed for use by Emma Bovary in hansom cabs. All cars,
whether adapted to petting or coition, have greenhouse-like
properties unless you live in a climate where the windows
quickly mist over. If you rely on condensation, it is still a good
idea to have a powerful light ready to dazzle cops or prowlers –
a really bright one will give you time to get dressed before their
sight returns.

For alfresco love, the least-screened parking site is the safest,
like a French eighteenth-century bower, because you can't be
crept up on. If you want to do much of this, buy a small van, or
one of those mini-campers known as adultery wagons, which
are in effect mobile houses. It takes confidence to strip naked in

rocking chair

Normally you sit astride facing, but other positions are possible.

any of these. For security, the best ploy is to make it a foursome, taking it in turns while the other couple drive, or sit stonily in front behaving themselves and providing cover. Mutual masturbation while driving, and trying to score the number of orgasms per gallon, are popular fantasies, but against the interests of safe driving. Seatbelts can be worn, or you can tie the non-driving party to his or her seat, and approach your work slowly.

motorcycle

Sexual venue which combines the symbolism of the horse with leather gear, danger, and acceleration. Has serious safety drawbacks, calls for the wearing of a hard hat, and you can't rely on the machine to look after itself as a horse can, but if you have access to a private road the hazards are yours. Better not attempted on the public highway. Another limitation comes from the fact that the passenger, male or female, sits behind, and you can't, or shouldn't drive with one on your lap – clothed or not. Probably better therefore as a preliminary to love than a venue for it unless you're prepared to do it with the bike on its stand. Don't let her liking for increased G override your judgment. Nobody looks virile dead.

horseback

Intercourse like this is attributed to the Tartars, gauchos, and other equestrian peoples. We haven't tried it, lacking the horse and the privacy. He controls the horse, and she sits astride facing him. If you were really set on this you could – in town – try a large rockinghorse, but whether it is worth the trouble we simply don't know. Quite a few women can get an orgasm when riding (especially bareback) and when jumping.

remote control

It is an old story that you can seduce a complete novice, who has no idea what you mean, by slipping a thumb into a closed fist, or between your lips, and absent mindedly moving it in and out, in and out. We'd like to see this. All of the people we have seen it work on have known very well what it was all about.

This is one version of the *pompido telecommando*. The lip one works better, nail downward in the appropriate rhythm – she will feel it where she should. She can do the same "at" him, for example in eating. Once habituated to either of these tele-control devices, most women and some men can be radio-controlled as to excitement, erection, and even orgasm – even by rubbing the lobe of one's ear – from several places down a table, the opposite side of a room, or the opposite box at a theater. The funniest use we've seen of this was when the lady was dancing with someone else, who spotted what was going on in his arms, but thought he was the source of the signals – which actually came from her lover, who was sitting out.

The original telecommando is the "blower" which connects the restaurant with the kitchen downstairs. Appropriate.

horseback
Quite a few women can get an orgasm when riding, especially bareback.

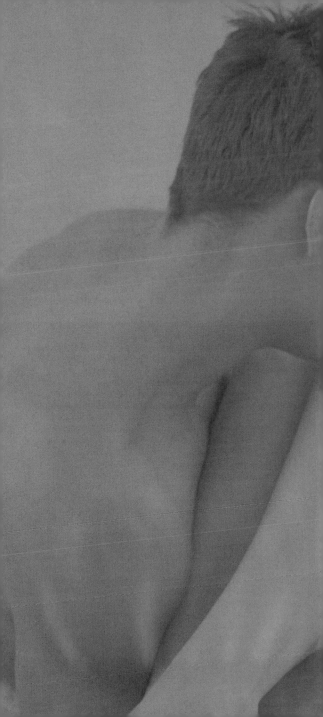

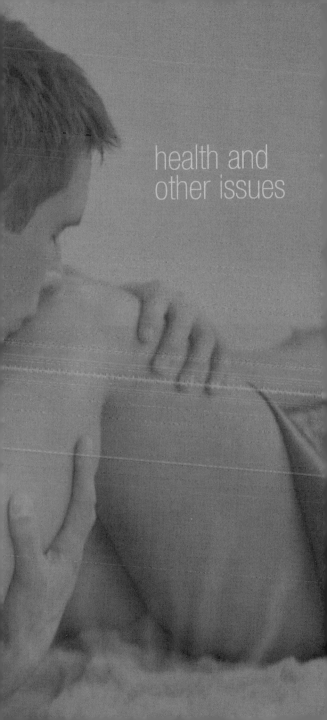

health and
other issues

AIDS and other sexually transmitted diseases

At the time when this book first appeared, it was a tenable view that as sexually transmitted diseases were declining overall, and the most dangerous of them were curable, they should not be major considerations in determining sexual behavior. That is no longer true. The appearance of the HIV virus (the precursor to AIDS), which are both currently incurable and fatal if not treated, has totally altered STDs' role in determining what we do sexually.

STDs have been covertly cited for several generations by straight society as God's punishment for sin. On the other hand, they are a real hazard of having intercourse, or heavy petting, with people you don't know. When we first wrote this book, the two most common sexually transmitted diseases were gonorrhea ("clap") and syphilis. Both are still around, but today the most common appear to be chlamydia (non-gonococcal urethritis), genital herpes, and trichomoniasis ("trich"); the gravest, outweighing these by far, is AIDS.

AIDS is caused by the human immunodeficiency virus (HIV). The virus dismantles the body's natural immune system to such a degree that it cannot fight off opportunistic infections such as pneumonia and tuberculosis, or cancers such as Kaposi's sarcoma and lymphoma. It can take up to 10 years for HIV to develop into full-blown AIDS, during which time the person infected may have no symptoms of disease.

Although there is currently no AIDS vaccine and no cure, the progress of the disease can be slowed with new retroviral drug combinations and any infections treated with high-dose antibiotics. Even so, although recent statistics show there has been a 70 percent drop in people who are being treated with the combination therapy, the drugs are still extremely expensive and most sufferers in the developing world have no access to such treatment.

It is too soon to assess the effects of these drugs long term – many of those already taking them experience an unpleasant raft of side effects, and there is always the fear of a new drug-resistant strain of HIV emerging. When a vaccine does become available, it may protect the uninfected, but not necessarily cure those already infected.

HIV is transmitted via bodily fluids, i.e. blood, semen, and vaginal secretions, the most common transmission route being through sexual intercourse, especially anal sex. But as it is a blood-borne virus, any activity which allows blood to pass from one person to another, such as injury, shared needles in intravenous drug use, or receiving contaminated blood products, carries a potential risk of infection. A woman can pass the virus to her unborn child, during the baby's birth or via breast milk.

Although AIDS first showed up in American gay men, it has now been shown that AIDS had lain undetected in Africa for decades. It is thought that post-colonial urbanization, new highways, and economic migration throughout Africa, which eroded traditional sexual mores and created new opportunities for sexual license, were at the root of the initial spread of the disease. It then made its way from the larger African cities to the rest of the world through sexually active visitors – homosexual, heterosexual, and bisexual. Although gay men and drug users still make up the bulk of people suffering from AIDS in Western industrialized countries, in sub-Saharan Africa, where nearly a quarter of the adult urban population is HIV positive, the spread of the disease is almost entirely through heterosexual contact. The majority of new infections worldwide is in African heterosexuals, with more than ninety percent of people with HIV today living in developing countries.

We have come a long way since the days of panic among the gay community, followed by a more limited panic among heterosexuals, when people thought you could catch AIDS from spitting, kissing, or shaking hands with an infected person. And mercifully we have moved away from the prejudiced belief that AIDS is a crime rather than an illness. But what worries AIDS researchers today is that we have now become too complacent. Young people in the West tend to think of it as an older person's disease, or one which can now be cured, and sexually transmitted diseases of all kinds – painful, embarrassing, and infectious – are once again on the increase.

The main point for anyone who is sexually active to take on board is that HIV can affect anyone, whatever their sexual orientation, race, or social group. We cannot afford to be reckless, or hide behind the comforting illusion that AIDS is someone else's disease. Anyone who has unprotected sex with someone whose HIV status is in doubt is potentially at risk. And because the virus can lie dormant, without showing any adverse signs of illness in the infected person for up to 10 years, many of us are not aware that we are infected.

If your newly found love won't use a condom, you are in bed with a witless, irresponsible, and uncaring person. Love "under the influence" is particularly risky – it makes you temporarily witless, irresponsible, and uncaring. The condom test is a good way of knowing whether or not you've found a decent, sensible partner.

A latex condom with a water-based lubricant such as K-Y jelly is safest for both vaginal and anal sex. (Oil-based lubricants like vaseline and baby oil destroy latex.) Have the condom in place from beginning to end of sexual contact, and use a new condom for each new act of intercourse, removing it carefully from the base of the penis after ejaculation. Store unused condoms away from heat and sunlight, don't keep them past their sell-by date, and beware rips and tears from fingernails. Used this way for every sexual encounter, condoms are a highly effective protection against all types of sexually transmitted diseases.

Some people find that using a spermicide, such as nonoxynol-9, which is found in contraceptive foams and pessaries, is an added protection against HIV. But it should only and always be used in conjunction with a condom. However, some research suggests spermicide is uncertain in helping prevent HIV transmission, and nonoxynol-9 may cause irritation that could actually promote the transmission of disease through broken skin.

The female condom, a thin, loose-fitting polyurethane pouch that lines the vagina and external sexual organs, is potentially a very effective protection against STDs because it includes the external organs. However, many partners don't like it, and many women find it difficult to insert and noisy when in use. Dental dams, thin latex squares to cover the female genital area, are a sensible precaution for anyone wishing to have safe oral sex with a woman whose HIV status may be in doubt, as vaginal secretions are a common vehicle for infection.

Testing for HIV, if you are worried you have been exposed to infection, is done by analyzing a sample of blood for HIV antibodies. Because antibodies are produced to fight a particular virus infection, their presence indicates the presence of the virus also. You need to wait six months between when you suspect infection took place and testing, otherwise your blood may show a false negative. Remember to practise safe sex in the interim. It is wise to talk to an AIDS counselor before being tested, so that you will have emotional preparation and support in the event you test positive, but also so that you are aware of other personal implications, for example, your future insurance and employment status. If you are unfortunate enough to test positive, you will also need counseling from the AIDS support services to help you with managing your sex life in the future. Even if you and your partner are both HIV positive, it is wise to use a condom during sex, as the virus makes you more vulnerable to other sexually transmitted infections such as herpes and chlamydia.

To sum up, anyone wishing to avoid all forms of sexually transmitted disease will 1) avoid unprotected sex, including oral sex, with all new sexual partners on all occasions; 2) avoid unprotected sex with anyone whose HIV status may be in doubt, including long-term partners if they are engaged in sexual relations with other people or high-risk activities such as intravenous drug use; 3) when using a condom, make sure you use it properly, i.e. wear it from the start to finish of any sexual encounter, use water-based lubricant, not oil-based ones, use a new condom for each new sexual act, remove the condom carefully after ejaculation, and store your condoms so that they are in good condition when you need them; 4) remember that the HIV virus is no respecter of race, sexual preference, age, or social position, so anyone you meet could potentially be carrying the virus, even someone who has never had sex before, or someone who tested HIV negative two months ago; 5) and finally, if you suspect you might have put yourself at risk of contracting the virus, be responsible. Inform any sexual partners, and avoid passing it on to anyone else.

Of other prevalent venereal diseases, NGU (non-gonococcal urethritis) behaves almost exactly like gonorrhoea but is due to the trachoma organism, not the gonococcus (one can catch both in a single dose), and accordingly it calls for a different antibiotic regime. Before the advent of HIV, genital herpes was blown up into a panic by interested parties. True, it can recur painfully in some people, exactly as its humbler cousin the cold sore can recur, and both are "incurable", i.e. you can't eradicate the virus with drugs. On the other hand, herpes is most infectious only when the blisters are present, and in the vast majority of people it is self-limited, the attacks getting l ess and less frequent over 3–5 years. A number of newer drugs are effective in cutting down the severity of the attacks. Herpes is mainly of concern in pregnancy, because an attack during labor can injure the baby. There is also a greater risk of cervical cancer in women who have herpes. Like other STDs, it makes infection with HIV more likely if the sufferer is exposed, and makes a person more likely to transmit HIV if they are a carrier. As with all venereal infections, refer this one to your doctor early. It is unclear why, media campaigns apart, herpes suddenly became prominent, for it is not a new disease.

Neither is trichomoniasis — this is an irritating vaginal infection with discharge ("whites") which has been endemic in the past (most women in some times and places had it chronically) and which is not always spread by intercourse. It can be caught from a partner because the male is a symptom-free carrier: in treating it, both partners have to be medicated to avoid reinfection.

Other STDs which are on the increase are human papilloma virus, which causes genital warts and, like herpes, increases the risk of cervical cancer, hepatitis B and C, and chlamydia. Chlamydia is of particular concern because, like HIV, there are often no real symptoms until the condition is well advanced, when vaginal discharge or abdominal pain may be present. And although this bacterial infection is easily and completely cured with a course of antibiotics, if untreated it can cause pelvic inflammatory disease (PID) and scarring to the fallopian tubes which, particularly in younger women, can result in permanent infertility.

Gonorrhoea and syphilis are still with us. Gonorrhoea is getting harder to eradicate because of the appearance of resistant strains: syphilis still responds quickly to penicillin. Don't in either case attempt to treat the disease yourself with antibiotics: don't cover up, and have the decency to warn your partner or partners. If it were not for the aura of magic, either of these diseases would be preferable to severe influenza or adult measles, because they are curable. All these, and other STDs, are becoming endemic in many developing countries and in the developing urban populations of developed countries, hand-in-hand with the HIV epidemic.

health and doctors

If you're acutely ill, you probably won't feel like sex. There are very few longer lasting medical conditions where a prescription of "no sex" is justified for more than a shortish time, like getting over a heart attack or a hernia operation, or, of course, if you have a sexually transmitted disease or are pregnant and likely to miscarry. Most doctors know this, but a few still give alarmist or thoughtless "no sex" instructions and are all the more likely to do so if their own sex lives are unimportant.

If the doctor advises the woman to avoid sex, she should find out why. He may only mean that pregnancy would be dangerous. The same applies if there's a heavy genetic risk. In that case, a thoughtful male partner would have a vasectomy, to be one hundred percent sure. Otherwise the only indications are the ones we've given. If it's the man who gets the red light, discuss it. Even severe heart or kidney illness isn't normally a bar to having gentle sex, nor is hypertension. In these cases, it might be sensible to avoid very tense or violent activities. Excitement is greatest, and casualties highest, in extramarital rather than married contexts, and boudoirs and brothels have seen more fatal accidents than the marriage bed. There can be a problem over cancer of the prostate or high blood pressure, because some of the drugs used to treat these can affect potency, and if other types of drug fail to work you may have to make a choice.

The important thing is not to take no for an answer unless you've had a full explanation and are sure the doctor knows how much sex means to you (some doctors still think that sex over the age of 50 is expendable or non-existent – see *Age*). A good doctor will know that stopping sex for any length of time is hard for normal people, and can damage an older man's sexual response when he tries to restart.

Really good and informed medical advice, by contrast, may be precisely what could help you to keep going and avoid further illness – you and the doctor should work out the solution together. Some people feel that if the worst came to the worst, it's the best way to go, and the anxiety and depression engendered by a ban on sex could be more likely to do harm than the very moderate exercise involved in intercourse. There is evidence that an improved sex-life can actually lower hypertension where this is due to general anxiety.

There is no special reason why doctors should advise us on sex techniques, but traditionally they often have done so. In fact, Avicenna wrote that it was a highly reputable part of their job, because pleasure in sex is "pertinent to generation". We'd probably say that it's also pertinent to being a whole person. In view of the clutch of health worries about sexuality which we still inherit, the doctor would be a very good counselor if he knew anything about it. In the past, particularly the Victorian past, medicine collected superconformists with all their age's anxieties and superstitions, plus a line of omniscient homespun moralism which is still with us, occasionally, over things like abortion and the Pill. This isn't the reason, however, that so many people, not only with problems, but simply, with straight questions about sexual matters, draw a blank from their physician and write either to magazines or to total strangers.

The trouble is that normal human sex behavior still isn't always taught. Until pioneer researchers such as Masters and Kinsey published their work, it couldn't be taught because there was only folklore to teach. When we were medical students in the 1940s, not even birth control was on the syllabus, though at least we were urged to read Havelock Ellis. Also most of what was in the textbooks was tendentious bunk. The sort of folk commonsense which used to figure in ballads and stories had gone, and so had the worldly wisdom of eighteenth-century doctors like John Hunter. Accordingly, with the best will in the world, a doctor who wanted to counsel on sex behavior either had to research it first himself, or read it out of one of the books, or go on his own experience – the last of these was fine if the experience was varied, but it could be limited, or eccentric, or absent.

This has changed with each generation, along with the change in cultural attitudes, though some doctors are a little inclined to realize their lack of background and push quite simple matters off onto the psychiatrist, who isn't necessarily any better qualified.

However, sex problems, especially if they involve health or, anxiety, or you can't get answers from books, are well worth taking to your doctor. If you are making a choice, a young doctor who talks your language or an older man or woman with some personal experience (if you can gauge this) is the best bet. If you have a bad problem and get no joy, persist; if the doctor you consult is hostile or embarrassed, change doctors. Shop around – medicine includes all sorts, and you don't have to put up with a Hippocratic oaf.

It's unfair to your doctor to be shy of letting him know, for example, if you have potency problems (they could be due to medicine he or she ordered, or explain a lot of other symptoms you've been getting); or to be unnecessarily reticent about your sex life generally, any more than you are about your digestion, problems with sleeping, or back pain. If you don't trust your doctor, he or she can't help you, and you ought to change doctors.

bidet

This article of European bathroom furniture used to be necessary when post-coital douching was the rule, but the Pill has altered that.

For washing, however, bidets can be useful, for example for cleaning your feet, and less trouble than a shower, though a woman looks better showering than sitting on a bidet like a battery hen. Indiscriminate douching is medically a bad idea in any case – the vagina is self-cleansing, and water merely upsets its natural hygiene. Keep the douche, and the bidet, for cleaning up after menstrual periods.

naked apes

We put a lot of biology into this book; too much exposition has been devoted to symbolisms in human sex behavior from a psychoanalytic standpoint which assumes, like old-style morality, that there is only one way of making love and only one thing it ought to express, and which is being superseded by biology. Work on monkeys suggests that, for humans, the possibility of prolonged and sensuous sex is something special, i.e. a "displacement activity", which enables all kinds of aggressions and anxieties, as well as infant deprivation of skin sensation to be worked out play-fashion in the context of mutual affection. Most people have at least one preferred sex behavior which a judge would find odd. If we saw these behaviors in fish or birds, we wouldn't ask whether they were normal, but what they were for. No writer who has watched apes could say, as one psychoanalytic author did, that any voluntary movement in sexual intercourse is evidence of latent sadism – if it is, then "latent sadism" means using sex to dissipate natural aggression in play. Problems only arise when the natural play-function isn't able to dissipate deeper anxieties. One of the tasks of research and counseling – the chief one – has been to dissipate successive layers of nonsense about sex written by each new generation of experts, and get back to the realities of human behavior.

Man's chief differences from most apes are pair-formation, the extensive use of sex as social bonding and play, shift of interest from brightly colored buttocks to breasts (one baboon has this too), and imagination. Well-known ape residues are blushing – all that is left of the mandril's red facial sex-skin (it happens all over to many women in orgasm, as a spotty-looking rash), and persisting buttock interest, which may include reddening them by smacking. Worth knowing only because sex is more fun, and preferences less alarming, if they make sense as natural history. Apes, like humans, masturbate and play bisexual games.

virginity

Have a bit of respect for this. The first time doesn't so much "matter more" to a woman than to a man, but it matters differently. If you find yourself getting into bed with a woman who is a virgin on only a few hours' or minutes' acquaintance, you're going too fast for both of you. Stay with the non-coital extras until you're both quite sure you know what you are doing. Cutting notches is irresponsible. Whatever you do be gentle and slow, as she's bound to be tense and nervous – even if she doesn't look it.

Women who are virgins will usually say (you can't tell reliably by inspection) and a loving man will ask. Men don't usually advertise the fact, but, however experienced he seems, the idea should be in the back of the woman's mind that this could be his first time and he may need help: if you're critical or disappointed you could do real mischief. If you're both virgins, you are starting from scratch – don't hurry it.

There's usually no physical problem over first intercourse if you're careful – the most common is simply male over-eagerness or nervousness (see *Impotence*). If there are problems, get them dealt with at once.

Defloration used to be a major obsession of past ages, but has stopped being a problem at all. There was a time when it was a constant preoccupation for the promiscuously minded male and a real worry to most girls. The change can't be due to the shortage of virgins (there has to be a first time for everything) nor even to the invention of lubricating jelly – it more probably is due to petting (perhaps) and a change in sexual folklore (certainly). Most girls are better educated and don't grow up on the tales of blood, sweat, and tears that their great-grandmothers used to tell. In the eighteenth century, a girl was disgraced if she didn't bleed like a pig on her wedding night; most modern lovers would reckon not to make her bleed at all unless she asks to be "deflowered" boisterously in the good old-fashioned way. Even then, unusual anatomy apart, it shouldn't hurt her "more than it hurts a vain young miss to get her ears pierced".

With the bogey of real defloration exorcized we can revive the eighteenth century play-wise. The Houris in heaven grow new hymens daily and are perpetually virgin, but so is every woman if she likes to pretend she is. It's not a bad way of celebrating an anniversary. Real enthusiasts can do the whole thing properly, honeymoon hotel and all; the result usually works far, far better than a real first-shot honeymoon. One can even book the same room in advance. Or one can do it oftener, at home, and at shorter notice. All she need do is to say, "Tonight, I'm a virgin."

frigidity

This does not mean failure to enjoy sex when one is dead with fatigue, when children are hammering on the door, in the middle of Union Square, or, generally, with the wrong man, at the wrong time, all of the time every time, or with the wrong vibrations. Males of the vending machine type (put in a coin and an orgasm comes out) should take note of this. Nor does it mean failure to get a mind-blowing orgasm on every single occasion. If it does mean these things, every woman is frigid.

Nor does it really apply to non-response if the man is clumsy, hurried, and phallus-struck. We assume you know all this.

Real frigidity is when a woman who loves her man and isn't consciously scared of any part of sex still fails to enjoy it when they've both taken trouble to see that she should. This condition, unlike male impotence, which can often be removed by simple reassurance (though not always), isn't easily helped by books. Female sexuality is much less arranged in a straight line than male – where a woman has difficulties of this sort, they have to be dealt with on an individual basis.

A few cases of non-enjoying are simple. The Pill can produce big swings in libido either way. So can the woman's own internal chemistry, which is cyclical, unlike the man's, and undergoes more sudden changes. If intercourse hurts, that is simple too – see a gynecologist and have it attended to. Pregnancy and having a baby can affect response, physically and psychologically. Assuming it's none of these, and you have a partner whom you can talk to and fantasize with, and you've eliminated obvious turn-offs like having an overweight lover on top of you, but still nothing really leaves you feeling satisfied, get personal advice. The mix of physical and psychological causes which can produce this kind of dissatisfaction is too complicated to be dealt with in a book.

The only technique worth trying, if you still don't feel satisfied, is painstaking self-education through relaxed, gradual, and private self-exploration. Masturbation in women is far more a process of continuing self-exploration than it is in men, and many women can and do teach themselves to respond in this way. On widespread testimony, the use of a vibrator helps – it can produce some sexual feeling in almost any woman. Once you have found a stimulus which makes you feel at all, whether you discover it solo or with your lover, incorporate it into lovemaking and use it to the full. If you need a finger on the clitoris, or genital kissing, use them fully – the propaganda about "vaginal orgasm" is propaganda, and there is no truth in the value judgment that unless you are fully satisfied only by deep penetration you aren't a woman; some women are satisfied by it, others aren't. Some women get many orgasms – some so many that they merge and can't be pinpointed as a single event – others get one, like a man. Some women only enjoy breast stimulation or genital stimulation. Find your pattern. If you haven't experimented with changes of posture, do – by this time we assume you have. And with play and fantasy. If none of these things gives you any lead you can develop, you need individual help (or more correctly help as a couple – if you see a counselor, both of you should go).

For self-training, start by getting really comfortable – naked or not, in front of a mirror or not, just as you prefer. Think and fantasize about anything which stirs any sort of response, then begin gradually to explore your own body, letting your hand go where your body wants it – breasts, the whole skin surface, labia, clitoris. Do the same if you use a vibrator – don't go for orgasm, but set out to discover what you like and what you

frigidity
Once you've found a stimulus which makes you feel, incorporate it into lovemaking and use it to the full.

think you would like. It takes time to learn this if you don't already know. Sometimes, if this doesn't frighten you or turn you off, another woman can help more than a man. That doesn't make you a lesbian. Don't assume that another man will be able to do better than your lover – he may, but it isn't a safe assumption. If you can imagine a situation which would excite you, try to set it up with your lover – as play, if it isn't feasible in earnest – remembering that fantasy-rape isn't real rape or fantasy-cruelty real cruelty. See if any of our suggestions turn you on in prospect. Talk to your man. Beyond that, we can't help through the printed page. Female libido is controlled, oddly enough, by the male hormone. See *Impotence*.

children

Children are a natural though not a necessary consequence of having sex. They impose responsibilities – not least those of being willing to stay together and rear them, and of having to restrict one's immediate sexual spontaneity for several years. For most people, they are well worth these restrictions, but, if you aren't prepared to accept the restrictions, don't have them.

Full-blooded sex is not exclusive to the childless, but if you want it you must arrange your own privacy. Never involve children in adult sexual activities: militant and exhibitionist liberals who try to acclimatize children to the naturalness of sex by letting them in at any level on their own sex lives probably do at least as much harm as was ever done by the prohibitive sex-is-dirty generation. It is possible for your children to see that love and sex are good from their awareness that your relations outside the bedroom are unanxious (if they are anxiously demonstrative, you will transmit the anxiety). What happens in other cultures is no guide here, because our society lacks their other supportive and educative mechanisms.

Most young children are biologically programmed to interpret the sight or sound of adult coition as evidence of a violent assault (they are aware of it earlier than you would expect, so don't keep babies in the bedroom), and the awareness of mother–father sexual relations is on all counts far too explosive a matter to be monkeyed with in the interest of Reichian experiments. Treating their own sexuality (masturbation, interest in the other sex, and so on) with acceptance and naturalness is a different matter, but don't push encouragement to the point of incestuous interference with their private lives, either in toddlerhood or in adolescence, or you'll end up trying to use them to enact your own unrealized fantasies and turn them off altogether.

Good sex education starts with being unbothered but not exhibitionistic, respecting your children's modesty, answering their questions, and letting them see that you regard this as a topic for pleasurable interest, naturalness – and privacy, not secrecy. Arrange the privacy with an eye to the fact that a normal toddler sees you as a rival, i.e. don't just lock him or her out.

Modern housing makes these counsels of perfection unless you are rich, but if you aren't prepared to make the necessary concessions, stick to having sex and don't have children. Nudity is another matter with which militant liberals can embarrass their children – there is a whole built-in biology of toddler response to adult parental genitals: we would say, "don't push it." Children should not be made to feel anxious about nudity. Some parents normally and unanxiously go about naked; but any element of a special educational parade is probably a bad idea.

The good thing about family attendance at nudist clubs is that the nudity of people in general lacks the biological and psychological anxiety overtones of nude parents, but don't push this either, and don't be surprised or discouraging over modesty among your offspring you don't as adults share. Don't forget that father's penis is a dominance signal and mother's vulva an ambivalent object to the normal 3- to 7-year-old boy. If you are being deliberately emancipated, you're probably overdoing it.

Preadolescent children should be told about normal sexual phenomena such as menstruation or masturbation before they happen, and before more anxious advisers (clergy, teachers, and other children) get there first – present them as what they are, part of the process and privilege of growing up: all sexual enlightenment, including where babies come from and the nature of intercourse, is best given even before it can be understood, so that the child grows up knowing what is what, and and is protected from scaremongers.

Egging adolescent children into sex experience is pathological. By that age, the test is whether they trust you and are sure enough that you will talk sense to ask your advice, but don't be shocked if they still keep their own counsel. If you are anxious or see trouble, say so frankly and directly, but don't bully. If you've done the job properly and your kids are endowed with reasonably good personalities, they will have no less sense, if less experience, than you have. A friend of ours found condoms in his 13-year-old daughter's possession and phoned the parents of her best friend "to warn them". Questioned by her father, the best friend said, "Yes, I know: I bought them for her. She's going with a boy, she wasn't taking precautions, and I didn't want to see her in trouble!"

Parents whose sex life is really unanxious will probably be good parents in this respect, but in our culture they are fairly rare, and we can't help our anxieties. Not much point in trying to hide these (many of them are built-in), and play-acting, whether moralistic or enlightened, is bad education and is seen through by children. If you are seen to be honest about your own feelings, that is as good as you are likely to get.

Finally, anyone who deliberately sets out to use a child or a pregnancy to prove something, to "keep the marriage together", or to boost their ego, needs to think again. Of course, children are ego-boosting and having them is a natural part of being a person, but they are people, not psychiatric procedures.

Adoption agencies are on the lookout for those who regard a child as a medicine, a medal, or a missile, and screen them out. If we could cut out similarly motivated natural parenthood, it would make for less mental illness, as well as solving the population problem in rich countries.

normality

A nineteenth-century book about sex, unless it was meant for the (then rich) underground, would have started with at least a genuflection to what was and wasn't sinful. The next generation of medical books, and much counseling literature, switched to laying down rules about what is and isn't normal.

Tack "abnormal" onto a sexual taste and it becomes worrying. "Normal" implies that there is something which sex ought to be. There is. It ought to be a wholly satisfying link between two affectionate people, from which both emerge unanxious, rewarded, and ready for more. That definition includes the awareness that people differ wildly in what they need and in their capacity to be satisfied; more, statistically, than in almost any other measurable. Since sex is cooperative, you can cater to one another alternately to bridge gaps. Add to this that sex, for reasons built into the species, makes us uniquely anxious compared with other divergences of need or taste, and our culture is coming out of a period of moral panic into a re-awareness that there is nothing to fear. Accordingly, a lot of people are still, in their sexual assumptions, like the generation of Victorian children brought up to believe that green sweets were poisonous, and rice pudding was good for you because it was unpalatable: they need reassuring.

One trouble in the past was that because of censorship by those with the arrogance to believe their morals should apply to us all, many good sex techniques were simply unfamiliar, and worrying or disgusting for that reason. It is not much over a lifetime ago that Krafft-Ebing wrote a textbook in which he described every sexual routine he didn't himself enjoy as a named "disease", salting the narrative with examples drawn from very disturbed people. Even Freud, who recognized that all of us have not one but a whole sheaf of sexually important drives – so much so that nearly all our interests have some sexual overtone – regarded maturity in terms of a pretty rigid highway code. There was practically an examination in "maturity" to take at the end.

"Abnormal" accordingly means (1) unusual for the time and place – having intercourse ten times a day on a regular basis is unusual, but it happens. If you can, fine. Leonardo and Newton were statistically unusual. (2) Unusual and disapproved: it's abnormal in Papua to bury dead relatives, and abnormal in California to eat them. Yet lovers all over the world would like "to eat" one another, and the same idea underlies our most beautiful and moving religious rite. At the same time an

Englishman or an American who actually ate a dead relative would have to be pretty sick. On a less extreme level, many in our society are nervous of same-sex affection. In classical Greece, it was a fashionable pose – everyone did it who could. In our culture, the people who show exclusively this sort of response are those who must. (3) Unusual and handicapping: a slipped disk or a really worrying sexual obsession are abnormalities because they spoil life, for the owner and his or her associates.

Some sex behaviors are obviously odd, and restrict the range of enjoyment – like the man who could only get orgasm by getting into a bath of cooked spaghetti. He, however, liked it that way. Unless the behavior is criminal, psychologists now do not usually ask "Is this normal?" but "Why does this particular person need this particular emphasis?" and "Is this behavior (a) spoiling his chances of being a full person, (b) tolerable for society?"

In sum, we don't have a single "normal" pattern of sex behavior, but a bunch of responses, like the fingers of a hand. In most people in a given culture, fingers are of roughly the same lengths. Some people have one finger longer than usual – a few are unlucky enough to have one long finger and the others stunted. The difference here is that finger lengths are much more tightly programmed and vary much less than sex behaviors. Accordingly, if you must talk about "normality", any sex behavior is normal which (1) you both enjoy, (2) hurts nobody, (3) isn't associated with anxiety, (4) doesn't cut down your scope. Insisting on having intercourse only in the dark, in one position, and with as little pleasure as possible, which used to be the moralists' stereotype of normality, is a very anxious and limiting routine. Good, unworried lovers use all five fingers of all four hands.

frequency

The right frequency for sex is as often as you both enjoy it. You can no more "have too much" sex than you can over-empty a toilet cistern (see *Excesses*), though you can cut your fertility by having too many ejaculations, and you don't want to make intercourse such an anxious business that you have to stick to a daily schedule. Two or three times a week is a common rate. Many people have it much oftener. Some people do stick to a pretty regular schedule – others like intensive weekends at intervals. Much under twice a week suggests you could be getting more out of it, unless you know by experience that the lower frequency is optimal for what you want.

People who stick strictly to coital orgasm are usually opting for fewer climaxes than people who mix coitus with oral, manual, and other plays because these increase the number of climaxes most men can get in a session. You should devise your own mix, in the light of your own responses: if one partner needs more, the accessory methods are useful to supply their needs and match them to yours. Frequency falls off normally with age, but there is no age when you won't, on some special occasion, surprise yourself. Don't be compulsive about frequency (or worry if your friends say yours is lower than theirs). You aren't being scored. Realize there will be times when one of you just doesn't feel like it – through preoccupation, fatigue, etc. – and don't enforce a timetable on them or yourself.

excesses

Quantitatively, in sex, these don't exist – nature sees to that; the woman gets sore, the man can't go on. Medical and moral old wives have spent centuries teaching that sexual overactivity is debilitating – they were never so admonitory over excessive work or excessive exercise, and rarely over excessive eating, which is our second most dangerous hang-up at the moment, after cigarette smoking.

Sex is in fact the least tiring physical recreation for the amount of energy expended. If you are flat after it, suspect either your attitude toward it or (more commonly) secondary loss of sleep. Male lovers forget that women who work or run a home or both aren't as fresh, even though they are as willing, as the idle occupants of the oldstyle Ottoman seraglio. Women forget that, though sex is the perfect tension-relief for both sexes, preoccupation rather than physical fatigue can cause impotence, especially when it goes with a wholehearted wish to perform up to and beyond Olympic standards as a matter of personal pride. Different sleep needs and sleep patterns, unrecognized and unaccommodated, can really threaten a sexual partnership. Deal with all these things by speaking out – being really in need of sleep only looks like rejection or sulking to very insecure people who can't communicate with each other. Sex commonly makes women languorous to the point of sedation. It may make men the same, but some emerge boisterously productive – in the second case, get up, produce, and let her sleep after a suitable interval of shared quiet and love. At night there is no sleeping pill as good as violent and shared orgasm – active lovers don't need sleeping pills.

If ever you do run yourself into the ground, there's no temporary exhaustion a few hours' or days' rest won't cure. Contrary to some belief, plenty of sex makes better and better sex – it damps down over-fast orgasm without lowering the peaks: the terrific "high" after a separation doesn't depend on continence, but on reunion. You can both masturbate daily while apart and still get it. Frequent sex also preserves function long into old age – not only is it a habit, but hormone levels depend on it; so, therefore, do looks and vigor.

impotence

The basis of so much nonsense and anxiety that a few facts are in order.

1 All men are impotent sometimes – usually at a first or a hurried session with someone highly desirable whom they want to impress. The risk is proportional to the build-up. Can also happen domestically, quite without expectation or warning – often from some turn-off one isn't aware of. The only importance of these occasions is not to be thrown by them. The conventional male fantasy of being ready to perform anytime, anywhere is wholly neurotic and impractical. Only the totally insensitive are all-time fucking machines like a stud bull, and stud bulls, too, have their off days. Leave yourself a whole night for a first night – you should wake horny.

2 If impotence is persistent, the causes in seventy-five percent of cases are physical – the chief are diabetes, obesity, alcohol, circulatory problems, some nervous disorders, and some drugs prescribed for depression or for high blood pressure.

3 The other occasional cause of impotence is psychological – turning oneself off by apprehension about sexual performance. This is the exact analogy to the old man who became obsessed with whether he slept with his beard in or out of the bed and went crazy trying to remember, or the pianist who starts thinking about his fingers.

4 If you can ever get an erection (by masturbation, in sleep, or on waking), there is nothing physical the matter with the hydraulics.

5 Age has absolutely nothing to do with impotence unless it brings illness. Belief that one is aging and must run out of steam has. Normal male potency lasts as long as life. The only change is that spontaneous erection gets rarer, direct skin stimulation is needed, and orgasm takes longer to come. Impotence in old men is due to turn-offs, lack of health and sexual interest in a partner, attempts to perform too often, or the demands of a younger partner who sets them a proficiency test. These turn normal people off at any age. Another common cause is medication. But if impotence comes on late in life after a lifetime without problems, it calls for medical review.

6 Accordingly, persistent impotence means either that you are trying to perform against a specific physical problem or a turn-off – wrong scene, wrong partner, wrong vibrations, record attempts – or that you are turning yourself off by acting as if you were a spectator, not a participant, and worrying about how you are doing. This can start if you are badly put out over one of the off days mentioned in (1) above and can become a habit. Deal with it exactly as for *Hairtrigger trouble*, except that

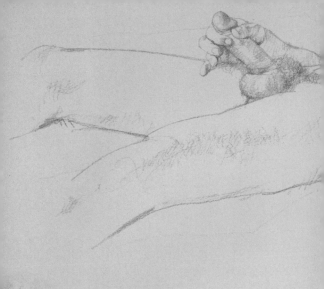

in this case both of you should use every accessory excitation, but with a firm resolve not to have intercourse – full description of the technique in Masters and Johnson which is easily adaptable to do-it-yourself. If this fails, get help from an expert. If everyone knew the facts listed here, the task of sex-therapists would at least be lightened by comprehension.

In the past, medical study of impotence was largely anecdotal. With recent research, it has become possible to measure penile blood flow, record the degree of erection which occurs during the R.E.M. (rapid eye movement) phase of sleep, and perform other investigations. One result has been to show that organic problems are more common than was realized: it used to be thought that 90 percent of erectile difficulty in people previously functioning was "in the mind", but this now appears an overestimate. After excluding diabetes, alcohol, medications, and hormonal disorders, there are still cases where erection is incomplete through a deficit in blood supply, "stealing" of blood by the muscular exertion of intercourse, filling defects in the hydraulics, or lax ligaments supporting the penis, making it bend. Accordingly, the route lies through excluding obvious causes, checking medication, following the regime indicated in (6) above, and then, if trouble persists, going to a sexual disorders clinic equipped to do proper investigations. In an ideal world, such units would be universally available – at the moment the best place to look is a teaching hospital.

Testosterone is not a universal aphrodisiac, and is not lacking in the vast majority of men who have erectile problems, though some physicians think that additional male hormone can lower the arousal threshold. Testosterone itself has the drawback of turning off your own internal hormone supply.

In impotent diabetics, and others with organic erectile problems, an alpha-blocking drug, phenoxybenzamine, can

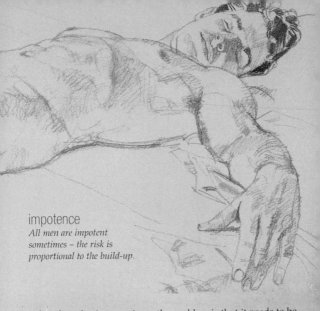

impotence

*All men are impotent
sometimes – the risk is
proportional to the build-up.*

produce long-lasting erection – the problem is that it needs to be
injected directly into the penile hydraulics. Injected papaverine
produces both immediate erection and some long-term benefit.
In real organic impotence, e.g. after extensive surgery, it is
possible to put a rigid support inside the penis, which renders it
serviceable. Whether it is worth the trouble and complications,
in view of the large range of enjoyable sexual behaviors which
don't require erection, and the fact that women rarely appreciate
the operative result, is a judgment call, depending on your
investment of self-esteem in penile rigidity.

In recent years Viagra – the little blue pill – has become the
drug of choice for male impotence. When it first came on the
market – having originally been developed for heart patients
who discovered a startling and gratifying side effect – the media
hailed it as a miracle cure. Taken an hour prior to intercourse, it
gives a good erection in approximately 60 percent of men,
provided the man is also sufficiently stimulated. It is said to
increase a woman's libido as well. However, like any other
stimulant, Viagra should be used with care. It should be
avoided by men taking nitrates for heart problems or who suffer
from retinitis pigmentosa. Side effects include headaches,
nausea, and blurred vision.

Important consequence of the fact that age alone doesn't
cause impotence is that its sudden onset with age in someone
previously functional is an indication for full medical
investigation, by a reproductive disorders clinic – not
resignation.

priapism

From Priapus, the Roman garden god with a large stiff wooden penis: erection you don't want and can't get rid of, unaccompanied by any feeling of sexual pleasure.

A painful erection which won't go away is rare, and is a medical emergency needing immediate attention, but is mercifully rare in humans. What is more common, though not common, is being woken at night by painful, non-pleasant erections, even when one has had a full ejaculation, so that the patient has to get up and walk around or shower – intercourse or masturbation does not help: the result can be severe loss of sleep. Mentioned here because the sufferers worry themselves gray about it. The cause isn't known – it may be psychological (it often stops away from home). All normal males get repeated erections in sleep, but usually these don't wake them or are accompanied by pleasantly sexy feelings, not pain. There doesn't seem to be a good remedy for this trouble. Drugs which turn it off are apt to turn off potency. Fortunately, the symptom usually goes away, and whatever treatment you were having at the time gets the credit. Does not interfere with sex at other times.

hairtrigger trouble

Alias premature ejaculation. Any ejaculation which happens before you both want it to is premature.

Premature coming results from two causes, over-eagerness and anxiety. Over-eagerness may be delightful on occasion, but usually means simply that you are not having enough sex to reach optimal performance. One can ward off this solo by masturbating frequently and using the occasion to develop slow responses, but in the presence of all the stimuli from a real woman this can still break down. Once you get anxious, it can become a physiological habit like stammering or impotence. It can rule out top-quality sex and most of our suggestions.

There is a set drill for handling this hang-up which rarely fails. Tackle it early.

1 Find out, with your partner, just how soon after one ejaculation you can get another erection, either by self-stimulation or with her stimulating you. Use this, holding back deliberately and aiming not to get an orgasm, but to see how long you can stay rigid. Do this often.

2 If the time interval is too long or you lose the second erection quickly, you need specific exercises. Set aside a time for practice and resolve that on the practice occasions you won't have intercourse. Get your partner to stiffen you, if necessary, and begin slow masturbation seated astride. Her aim will be simply to keep you in erection, even if she has to drop her stroke-rate to one in three seconds. If you call "stop" she must stop. She can tie you if

this really gives her better control, but as this itself is an excitant it is better if you deliberately hold still. Don't be worried if on the first occasion you ejaculate at once – try again half an hour later. Do this just as often as you can arrange it, but intersperse with intercourse, however short, so as not to build up an appetite. Either in intercourse or for practice sessions, some people find a local anesthetic jelly a help, and, if you find it difficult to get the exercises going, you could try this. In about three weeks of regular practice, you should be able to hold at least a second, and probably a first erection, for a full five minutes, and this will get longer and longer. Meanwhile, try to lengthen the straight coitus sessions. Use all the extras to give your partner full orgasm as often as she needs it, but she should be sparing with very stimulating techniques, or indeed any techniques, ahead of penetration. Try holding still inside her for timed minute intervals.

3 If this doesn't work, or you are getting anxious, see an expert. Usually it does work. The important thing is to set up by agreement a definite noncoital session, designed to get you into a state of sexual training. You will both benefit, and she needn't go without meanwhile: learn to use your hands and your tongue and don't forget her breasts. Having times when you specifically set out to satisfy her will help you to relax over any virility problems. If the problem remains, take advice before it gets to be a habit. Most men with limited sex experience are over-quick to start with, and would benefit from training of the kind we've described.

At the first session with a much-desired partner, at least 50 percent of men either ejaculate too quickly or fail to get an erection. Ensure a whole night, so you can try for a comeback, but don't try too hard. If you go to sleep, you will probably wake with a huge erection.

Note for your doctor: Tricyclic antidepressants such as Tryptizol (Rx) or Tofranil (imipramine, Rx) slow down orgasm enormously in some males without blocking erection: minute doses are often enough.

menopause

The time at which the woman ceases menstruation. Old John Fothergill, the Quaker doctor, wrote in the eighteenth century: "There is a period in the life of Females to which, for the most part, they are taught to look forward with some degree of anxiety: the various and absurd opinions, relative to the ceasing of the menstrual discharge, propagated through successive ages, have tended to embitter the hours of many a sensible woman – some practitioners, in other respects able and judicious, if they have not favored these erroneous and terrifying notions, seem not to have endeavored to correct them, with the diligence and humanity which such an object requires." That about sums it up.

Menopausal changes are complex. The end of ovulation means the end of fertility, and for some women this subtly affects their self-esteem, quite apart from any physical effects of a shift in hormone balance. For others it represents a sexual release, when they no longer need worry about contraception. While a few things, like irregular bleeding or hot flushes, are hormonal, personality changes like irritability and depression could be both hormonal and due to the fact that a milestone has been passed and one has stopped being young. Men, who don't have a menopause or any sudden hormone change, often undergo a "male menopause" which coincides with realizing what they haven't done among the fantasies of youth, and that they had better do it now. This can lead to injudicious thrashing about, actual illness, or simply reassessment of their aims and opportunities very like a second adolescence.

Sex life for women doesn't end with the menopause unless they have been convinced that it should or feel they are "no longer women". Often it really begins then, if pregnancy has been a worry.

Whether the symptoms are physical or mental, such as mood changes, hormones are often worth trying to ease over the readjustment (under medical supervision). Hormone replacement therapy (HRT), apart from the beneficial effects on bone health and for the small minority of women who suffer severe menopausal symptoms, is probably over-prescribed. There are quite extensive side effects for some women, which are not properly taken into account. Ask your doctor about natural alternatives that can have the same benefits. The Pill can obscure the menopause by altering or suppressing the cycle: don't stop it until you are sure you are not still ovulating, or you may get surprisingly pregnant. After the menopause, a few people need estrogen to combat dryness or soreness in intercourse – but continued sexual activity seems to work nearly as well as doctors' prescriptions in preserving the function of both sexes far into later life. See *Age*.

age

The only thing age has to do with sex performance is that the longer you love, the more you learn. Young people (and some older ones) are firmly convinced that no-one over 50 makes love, and it would be pretty obscene if they did. Ours isn't the first generation to know otherwise, but probably the first one which hasn't been brainwashed into being ashamed to admit it.

Some couples may be starting on some of our suggestions when they've been through the groundwork and reached their thirties. Since, however, we shall all get older, and superstitions still persist, it is worth giving the facts.

Neither men nor women lose either sexual needs or sexual function with age. In men, the only important changes over the first seven decades are that spontaneous erection occurs less often (accordingly they need more direct penile stimulation from the woman), ejaculation takes longer to happen, which is an advantage, and coital frequency tends to fall, but given an attractive and receptive partner, decent general health, and an absence of the belief that one ought to run out of steam, active sex lasts as long as life. In later life, the ability and need to ejaculate frequently get less. It's a good idea not to try for it every time, which will give you more mileage and no less mutual pleasure. Women lose their fertility at the menopause, but that in itself often helps rather than spoils their sex life. In fact, there is little if any physical decline in any attribute except frequency up to 75 and beyond. From a quarter to a half of all couples of this age still have regular sex, and that includes all of the people who never had much of a sex life when they were younger. Since continued activity keeps hormone levels up, for couples who make love often it's probably closer to 75 percent and the other quarter will have stopped because of arthritis or the other ills of age, not impotence or frigidity. "The things that stop you having sex with age are exactly the same as those that stop you riding a bicycle (bad health, thinking it looks silly, no bicycle)." The difference is that they happen later for sex than for bicycles. Over 50, the important thing is never to drop sex for any long period – keep yourself going solo if you don't for the time being have a partner: if you let it drop, you may have trouble restarting (see *Health and doctors*).

Women can, of course, be kept menstruating indefinitely with hormones. There's probably little point, unless it boosts morale. A few find they get dry vaginally and need some estrogen, but in fact the results of continued sexual activity and of hormone pills are just about equal.

As with so many things, later life is the time when you've tried everything, and settle down to the things you like most – together.

obesity

Fatness in our culture is unlovely, but in some cultures it is less of an issue, and for others it is a positive sign of health, prosperity and beauty. Renoir's women, who, when naked, look ideal for sex, would look a little too plump if clothed.

What isn't realized is that in men, being overweight is a physical cause of impotence. If neither this nor the esthetics of it bother you, you may still have to circumvent it. King Edward VII of Britain ("Tum-Tum"), had a special couch resembling a gynecological table made to enable him to get on target. Most stout men can manage with the woman astride, backing or facing. If this doesn't work, try lying face-up over the edge of the bed, feet on the floor, while she stands astride. An over-heavy man is a bad problem – Cleopatra could say, "O happy horse, to bear the weight of Anthony," but he didn't weigh 200 pounds. If you are grossly overweight, set about losing it,

212 HEALTH AND OTHER ISSUES

whether you value your sex life, or just your life. That applies to both sexes. Modern women, though supple, tend to be underweight by the sexual standards of the past, especially for rear-entry positions and for making love on a firm surface.

bisexuality

All people are bisexual – that is to say, they are able to respond sexually to some extent toward people of either sex. Being "homosexual" isn't a matter of having this kind of response, but usually of having some kind of turn-off toward the opposite sex which makes the same-sex response more evident or predominant: in some people, homosexuality is analogous to left-handedness and may have similar causes in brain function (which makes nonsense of it being "unnatural" or sinful). How far people act bisexually depends on many things, including the society they live in, their opportunities, and how far the same-sex part of their response worries them.

Being actively bisexual makes problems in our society, not least with the other-sex partner on whom most people's worthwhile sex life depends. It is difficult enough to have to make out with half the human race without trying to make out with the whole of it. Moreover today, although bisexuality is not "unnatural", as evidenced by the homosexual dreams all heterosexual people may occasionally have, and by what we know about primatology, a male who has been actively "bisexual" without practicing safe sex poses an active threat to partners because he may be HIV positive.

Medicine is concerned about this group because, together with people who have injected drugs or been given intravenous blood products, they spread HIV into the general sexual community. (Bisexual women don't present this risk unless they became infected incidentally, because AIDS rarely passes between lesbians; women far more readily respond to other women than men do overtly to men, because intimacy between women is socially acceptable, while anything looking like male–male affection has been tramped on with society's heaviest boots.)

Although the homosexual community has responded rapidly and intelligently to the threat by altering its sexual behaviors, a high proportion in some areas are, tragically, already infected. In consequence, the only safe male–male sexual activity is mutual masturbation. In threesomes and two-couple interactions, which were becoming more common and less taboo, an infected man can infect not only the woman, but even more probably the other man as well if he has intercourse with the same partner immediately before him, since semen is the vehicle for infection. Overtly bisexual men are a high-risk group, and both they and their partners of either sex need to be aware of this and take protective action. The course of action against contracting AIDs for anyone, no matter what their sexual orientation, is to avoid casual sex and always use a condom. This is tough, but becoming a carrier of a lethal disease is tougher still.

hazards

Contrary to superstition, very few sexual techniques are actually dangerous. Clumsy penetration with the woman on top can injure him or her, violent anal penetration can injure her, and any intercourse with a stranger carries a risk of AIDS. Women liable to miscarry need to be handled gently in pregnancy, and women who are very liable to miscarry might do better to avoid orgasm while carrying, especially in the first and last few weeks. Apart from these, there are a few tricks which are risky in themselves. None of these is popular, but clearly, since mischief is reported, people occasionally try them.

1 Never throttle anyone, even in play, and especially in orgasm. For women who treat partial strangulation as a kick, they can get exactly the same sensation safely by intercourse head down; see *Inversion*. Never block a partner's airway, and be extra careful with bondage games – one can suffocate on a soft surface.

2 Never blow into the vagina. This trick can cause air embolism and has caused sudden death.

3 In spite of writers who talk about the use of household appliances for sex kicks, never fool about sexually with vacuum cleaners or with air-lines. A garage tyre inflator line has ruptured the intestine when squirted 18 inches from someone's anus (this was a practical joke). Vacuum cleaner injuries of the penis are surprisingly common and very hard to repair satisfactorily. Water at tap-pressure is safe, but direct it at the clitoris, not forcibly into the vagina – anything under pressure can go up the Fallopian tubes and do harm.

4 Cantharides (Spanish fly) is not an aphrodisiac, but an irritant poison about as powerful as mustard gas. The dose which produces useless, painful erection by inflaming the penis is bigger than the fatal dose for kidney damage. Chocolate containing it has killed several women.

5 Nothing you inhale is a safe kick: organic chemicals which produce dizziness also produce death rather easily. Amyl nitrite produces flushing and other sexy sensations, but is grossly unsafe to fool with.

6 Like anal intercourse, mouth–anal contacts appear from recent work to be risky, and better avoided.

Considering the range of human sexual experimentation, it is a reflection on conventional fears that only manifestly idiotic sexual experiments are dangerous. Given reasonable gentleness, sex play is by far the safest energetic sport – one can be killed by a golf ball.

prostitution

Prostitutes don't as a rule either practice or enjoy advanced lovemaking. This isn't true for all professionals in all cultures, but in ours the commonest motive for becoming a streetwalker is economic. Prostitutes' attraction insofar as it persists is in part mythological, and also due to their unshocked understanding of unscheduled sex needs, the fact that the man can at least be sure of getting sex from them without social hang-ups, and a group of feelings connected with sharing a woman with other males.

No doubt if we treated the professional as other cultures have done – on a par with the concert artist who gives up domesticity in order to practice an art – the personnel of professional sex would improve, and it would lose its present psychopathology, and be of help both to bothered clients and to the women themselves, but general sexual freedom is more likely to displace monetary sex altogether, except for those for whom it arises from unconscious needs.

Apart from the attractions we've mentioned, any woman who herself is ready to enjoy and understand sex, and meet her partner's needs as fully as a professional, but with love, can outclass anyone hired. She can learn from periods and cultures in which the courtesan was a repository of the art of pleasing, but what we call whores' tricks ought to be called lovers' tricks. A woman who can make love with love and variety needn't fear commercial competition.

anal intercourse

In the light of present knowledge, this is best avoided altogether. It is something many couples try once, and a few stay with it, either because the woman finds it gives her intenser feelings than the normal route, or because it is pleasantly tight for the man. But it is the best method of catching, or transmitting, the virus of AIDS, as well as hepatitis, cytomegalovirus and intestinal infections, and it can also cause mechanical damage.

Initial attempts to render anal intercourse safer by using a condom were unreliable because the thin condoms designed for vaginal use tend to tear under the increased pressure and friction of a canal primarily engineered for other purposes. There are now stronger, more resistant condoms on the market, but, as long as AIDS remains incurable, it is still a risky activity.

The reason that AIDS is more easily transmitted anally than vaginally is that the rectal mucosa is not designed for friction and bleeds easily, so that semen can enter the bloodstream, and the rectum lacks the infection-resisting mechanisms of the vagina.

Anal sex has a chequered history. Regarded as an abomination because of its association in the public mind with homosexuality (though by no means all gays made use of it even before AIDS arrived), it has always been around. The Roman poet Martial threatened to divorce his wife for refusing, unlike other Roman matrons, to cooperate: in the 19th century, anal intercourse was a popular working-class contraceptive. How far the hazard element is due to a new virus and how far it was always present we do not know. It is certainly present now. There are not many popular sexual practices that are physically dangerous, but recent circumstances and the most recent medical knowledge indicate that this is one of them. When a hazard as serious as AIDS appears there is plenty of scope to avoid it by altering your sexual repertoire.

pain

Pain *per se* isn't a sexual excitant in spite of folklore. What actually happens is that once excitement starts to build, pain awareness is reduced steadily, until any strongish stimulus, even one which normally would be over-strong, adds to the build-up. This can be true elsewhere – you can lose a tooth in a football game and not notice it until after – but with sex excitement the pain-stimulus can actually be transformed into increased pleasure-feeling provided it isn't too strong. There is a sharp point, however, at which over-stimulation becomes a turn-off, not a turn-on, and if this is overstepped the build-up collapses: tolerance increases the closer you get to orgasm – just before it people can take, for example, quite hard slaps – but the transformation stops as soon as orgasm occurs, so don't continue awkward postures or hard stimuli after this. Some people don't transform at all. If anything you do is perceived as straight untransformed pain, it's either too much or too early on, or you've gone on after orgasm. Learning what stimuli are pleasant as build-up and what aren't is an art.

If any part of normal sex actually hurts, due to soreness, internal organs getting knocked etc., you're being clumsy or something is wrong – in the second case, see a doctor if it lasts more than a few days. First coitus can be slightly painful for both parties – if they are excited enough beforehand, the transformation effect will get most women through the pain barrier, though if she bleeds at all give time for abrasions to heal before the next round. If it's more troublesome than this, get advice (see *Virginity*). With gentleness and preliminary stretching it can be quite painless in most women.

Actual craving for pain (mental or physical) as a sex kick isn't uncommon. Usually, the idea is exciting in fantasy, but a turn-off in practice, unless your partner is skilled enough to keep inside the limits of transformation by excitement, and the fantasy itself isn't too violent. Many men who have persuaded a partner to "beat them hard" because the idea sounded exciting have been put off a repeat performance. If your partner has such fantasies, keep well inside their powers of stimulus-transformation, subtract a good twenty percent from the fantasy, and watch out for the occasional sick character who really enjoys the idea of being injured. For sane people, commonsense, a bit of play-acting, and intelligent use of the transformation effect can more than take care of the normal fantasy range.

fetishes

Something you need instead of, or as well as, a partner in order to reach full sexual response. Less often evident in women than in men, so far as concrete objects or routines are concerned, though women can make fetishes of such things as security, fear, and subtler nuances of setting. Can be of all kinds – embryo fetishes are present in almost everyone, and their satisfaction is part of the art as well as the function of love. Many men perform best with a woman who has a particular hair color or length, or big breasts, or looks boyish, but are less frank about other turn-on requirements. Particular garments come next – she is more desirable with stockings, or with shoes, or with earrings. Use any of these turn-on circumstances to their fullest extent (see *Clothes*).

A real fetish is any non-sexual circumstance which is obligatory for potency. It becomes a problem if it swamps everything and develops into a consuming anxiety (shoes only, not even women with shoes) or if it happens to be a fantasy which turns you on and your partner off, or if the performance gets more and more complicated and anxious until a halt has to be called. Normal marital play can meet nearly all demands of this kind if there is real communication, and find them fun, but the partner who is stuck with an anxious ritual can be a big problem which let's-pretend fails to solve.

For a start, a person with a real hang-up of this sort, even if fully enacted, can lose interest in anything but his preoccupation. This is a medical problem, however, and time to shout for help. It goes with other personality difficulties of which the loss of interest in love is only a symptom, since most of us at some level have one or more preferred turn-ons, and, if we can't communicate with our partner, tend to get more and more guilty and sensitive about them. Discharged as play, this doesn't happen; but if they can't be discharged in this way, get help. We're talking, remember, about persistent and quite inordinate obsessions which get in the way of the ordinary business of intercourse – refusing to try anything but the missionary position is as much a fetish as only being potent when wearing a diving helmet. Normal sex involves both fantasy preferences and variety – variety is the one thing the handicapped ritualist can't enjoy. There's not much wrong with anyone who is willing to try anything once.

It may sound brutal, but don't, repeat don't, take on a partner with a major sex problem or compulsive ritualism in order to "cure them by love". You won't – though if they have your love and comprehension, cure by an expert, or at least coming to live with themselves, will be much easier. If you have taken on a problem of this kind – and the measure, we repeat, of whether it is a problem is whether it causes anxiety and interferes with sexual joy – work it out between you without fear or recrimination, and go to an expert. It's as much a medical problem as a slipped disc if it interferes with your mutual enjoyment as much as a slipped disc would.

transvestitism

Many people enjoy dressing in each other's clothes on occasion for the hell of it. That isn't transvestitism. A transvestite is a person who, while staying fully in his or her own sex role, feels an intense compulsion at times to dress the opposite sex role, and an intense release of anxiety (not so much a kick) when they do so. They are not "homosexual", and a bisexual person who dresses the opposite sex to please a partner isn't a transvestite. A transexual is a person, usually male, who actively wants to turn into a person of the other sex, by surgery if necessary, and feels totally miscast as they are.

In some simpler societies, there are roles or ceremonies which discharge these needs (wizards often cross-dress). In our society, they can cause intense anxiety. A transvestite with an informed and unscared partner usually finds that his compulsion, whatever its cause, doesn't spoil his sex life in the male role (if he has to keep it secret or she thinks he's queer or crazy, which he isn't, he can get really sick from worry); a transexual needs expert help and may or may not be the happier for a sex-change operation. A lot of unhappiness could be avoided if people knew the facts to the point of not being scared or shocked if they come across them. If you have a partner with any of these problems, help them by comprehension and see they get help from an expert.

perversion

In books prior to the 1970s, this meant, quite simply, any sexual behavior which the writer didn't himself enjoy. More correctly, it means something antisocial which people use as a substitute for the sexuality from which their hang-ups debar them. The commonest perversions in our culture are getting hold of some power and using it to kick other people around, money-hunting as a status activity, treating other people, sexually or otherwise, as things to manipulate, and interfering with other people's sex lives to ensure that they are as rigid and as anxious about them as the interferer. Scheduled perversions like digging up corpses or committing lust murder are confined almost wholly to borderline psychopaths and, though obviously serious, are of less social importance than the respectable kinds because they are rare and disapproved of. It's a measure of the prestige of socially approved perversion that most public utterances in

legislation, law enforcement, and so on genuflect to what are
basically perverse attitudes, even when the speakers are
privately healthy.

Hang-ups of this sort are extremely difficult to cure.
However sorry you are for the possessors, they are dangerous
people and best avoided as partners or as mentors – you will
only be asking for a lot of trouble.

birth control

This is the discovery which more than any other made carefree
sex possible. Before that one had to be infertile to enjoy the kind
of extended sexual play which is now available to everyone. No
other method being wholly reliable, women who have
experienced the security of the Pill and discovered the play-
function of sex are not going to return to the old insecurity,
despite unfounded health scares in recent years. The Pill is still
the safest and best method, and a safer drug than aspirin.
Intrauterine devices (IUDs), which prevent implantation, don't
suit everyone, but work well for some. If you can't use these, it
is back to the cap plus a good chemical spermicide. Some
women find capping themselves before sex is offputting and
reduces spontaneity. Some also get resistance from their
partners (though if it is the only method she can use, don't
make a song and dance about it; that won't change anything
and will make her apprehensive); other women don't mind,
though both caps and spermicides can spoil both the feel of the
vagina and the genital odor, but usually not seriously. One point
about the Pill is that, by turning off the normal acid vaginal
secretion, it makes it far easier for some women to catch an STD
or thrush, even from very slight genital or oral contact.

Condoms are now the essential precaution, not just against
conception but also against AIDS. Everyone except long-term
exclusive lovers has to get used to using them on every occasion
– and the condoms should preferably be lubricated with
nonoxynol-9 (see *AIDS and other sexually transmitted diseases*).
Both sexes need to become really expert in handling condoms
without allowing leakage: they need to be removed before an
erection starts to subside, and the wearer should wash.
Condoms and the hygiene connected with them may be a
nuisance, but they are a lifesaving nuisance, and not all aspects
of their use are drawbacks. The very manipulation involved in
letting the woman put one on her man excites some people: thin
or "gossamer" condoms can slow down some over-quick
ejaculators. Uncircumcised men, and men with a pointed rather
than round-ended glans, can't usually use the teat-ended kind –
in this case ask for the round-ended variety. Some makes of
knobbed or otherwise decorated sheaths sold to vary vaginal
sensation are not reliable, or leakproof, so don't trust them.

As with AIDS, so with contraception – never take a risk.
The "morning after" pill has a high rate of effectiveness and

can be taken up to 72 hours after unprotected sex occurred. It can now be bought from your doctor or family planning clinic, as well as some pharmacies.

The so-called rhythm method ("Vatican roulette") doesn't merit serious consideration as it is highly unreliable.

Vasectomy is the one reliable, once-and-for-all male contraceptive method. It consists of closing off, by a small surgical operation, the tubes down which the sperms travel from the testis. The operation is done under local anesthetic. It hurts rather less than having a small cut stitched, and you can go straight home. The long-term result is a completely virile but infertile male. (Repeat, competent vasectomy carries absolutely no risk of physical interference with erection, ejaculation, sexual feelings, or virility generally; under the name of "Steinach's operation" it used to be done as a rejuvenation treatment and virility booster.)

If you have all the children you want, you should consider vasectomy seriously. Certainly consider it rather than allowing your woman to undergo the much bigger operation needed to sterilize her, or keeping her on the Pill if it doesn't suit her.

There are a few more factual points to consider.

1 Vasectomy doesn't make you sterile at once. Sperm can hang around for months, so you must stick to your previous birth control method until you know you are clear. Your doctor will let you know when you can both forget about birth control.

2 You can't easily change your mind. Vasectomy is sometimes reversible, but you mustn't count on that. It's a calculated risk that you might suddenly want to father children later, but not worth hanging back for if otherwise it looks right for you. It is now possible to store your sperm in a sperm bank prior to the vasectomy, for use at a later date should your circumstances change.

3 On the other hand, make sure you know your own feelings – which in any matter connected with sex and reproduction are never wholly reasonable. If the doctor refuses to do the operation "off the shelf" without discussing your general self-picture of maleness, that onlyshows that he knows his job. If your doctor refuses on principal or because he doesn't like your lifestyle, consult another doctor.

4 Vasectomy doesn't make someone who is HIV positive any safer as a partner: if you can ejaculate at all, you can spread the virus.

If you are in a long-term relationship and have the family you want, or don't want children, give vasectomy serious thought.

birth control
*The manipulation involved as
a woman puts the condom on
the man is exciting in itself.*

infertility

A boon if you want it, a curse if you don't. Can be due to the woman not ovulating, the ova not reaching the uterus through tubal blockage, various conditions in the female organs; the man not having any sperm, or enough sperm; and probably also various chemical incompatibilities between partners. These can sometimes be helped by advice including concentration on fertile periods, surgery, or hormones, but need proper medical counseling (both of you must go – if the man has too few sperm there is no point in subjecting the woman to a lot of investigation). Anxiety can sometimes apparently block fertility – over-frequent ejaculation lowers the sperm count, so don't be over-eager. Tight warm clothing around the scrotum can kill off the sperm, which need to develop below body temperature. Orgasm in the woman doesn't make conception more likely. Infertility can sometimes end suddenly after years, and the treatment or the life situation get the credit. Obstinate lack of sperm in the male is difficult to treat, though you can concentrate the sperm he has and inseminate with them with in-vitro fertilization. It has nothing whatever to do with virility judged by sexual performance. Never assume you are infertile unless it has been proved, and be careful stopping the Pill around menopause time. For voluntary infertility, see *Children, Birth control*.

termination

All ethics apart, neither you nor the doctor can be quite sure exactly how a woman – or a couple – will react to it psychologically.

Early abortion, due to recent medical advances, is now a less traumatic procedure, relatively speaking, than the old-style general anesthetic and surgery. The so-called "abortion pill" acts by causing an early miscarriage and is appropriate up to 14 weeks of pregnancy. The drug is taken under medical supervision, two days apart, but no hospitalization is required if there are no complications.

The other early abortion option is vacuum aspiration abortion. Again this is an outpatient procedure and can be done under local or general anaesthetic. After fourteen weeks, abortion is more difficult and more dangerous, and should be avoided wherever possible. Done too late it involves killing a potentially viable child.

If you plan your sex life properly and take informed, conscientious contraceptive precautions, you shouldn't need to terminate a pregnancy except on exceptional grounds. Odd that the main moral woe-criers on abortion are also the people who have done most to block proper birth control, and starve research and education about it of the funds they require.

index